His Redeeming Love

HIS REDEEMING LOVE

Jonathan Edwards

Compiled by
JUDITH COUCHMAN
and LISA MARZANO

SERVANT PUBLICATIONS
ANN ARBOR. MICHIGAN

Vine Books is an imprint of Servant Publications especially designed to serve evangelical Christians.

Compiled by Judith Couchman and Lisa Marzano.

Published by Servant Publications
P.O. Box 8617
Ann Arbor, Michigan 48107

Cover design: Alan Furst, Minneapolis, Minn.

00 01 02 03 10 9 8 7 6 5 4 3 2 1

Printed in the United States of America
ISBN 1-56955-112-X

Library of Congress Cataloging-in-Publication Data

Edwards, Jonathan, 1703-1758.
    His redeeming love / Jonathan Edwards ; compiled by Judith Couchman and Lisa Marzano.
        p. cm. — (Life messages of great Christians)
    ISBN 1-56955-112-X (alk. paper)
    1. God—Love—Meditations. 2. Devotional calendars. I. Couchman, Judith, 1953- II.
    Marzano, Lisa. III. Title. IV. Series.
    BT140 .E38 2001
    242'.2—dc21

                                                                    2001045459

For Deena Davis,
a loving friend

CONTENTS

Many thanks to the team at Servant Publications for supporting this book and the *Life Messages of Great Christians* series, especially Bert Ghezzi, the company's editorial vice-president. We're also grateful to our editor, Liz Heaney, for her contributions to this book.

We also thank those who prayed for the compilation process: Joan Badzik, Betty Bradley, Charette Barta, Jan Condon, Opal Couchman, Win Couchman, Kathy Fisher, Tammy Halliday, Madalene Harris, Karen Hilt, Shirley Honeywell, Karen Howells, Linda Kraft, Mae Lammers, Nancy Lemons, Beth Lueders, Marian McFadden, Cindy Miller, Victoria Munro, Kay O'Connor, Arlene Ord, Rita Rocker, Naomi Smith, Connie Swanson, Mary Jane Tynan, Lucibel VanAtta, and Kathe Wunnenberg.

In a high school English class I gobbled up early American literature, but only the essence of a few works actually lodged in my memory. One was an excerpt from the sermon "Sinners in the Hands of an Angry God" by the Puritan preacher Jonathan Edwards (1703–758).

Though my teacher labeled Edwards' treatise antiquated and irrelevant for today, it deeply affected me. If God really was mad at sinners, I was in trouble. Being a sensitive type, it didn't take much to convince me of my inadequacies, and I could practically feel this wrathful God breathing down my neck. For years afterward I thought of Edwards as "that angry preacher" and steered clear of all things Puritan. I didn't want to feel guilty.

Unfortunately, my encounter with Edwards as a teenager told only part of his story. Yes, Edwards did preach about sin and hell, but that was not all. He also spoke of God's love for and redemption of sinners, and rarely were these truths separated from his warnings about eternal punishment. His basic message was simple but profound: Though we sin and deserve divine retribution, God has provided a way of rescue through His Son, Jesus Christ. If we accept God's free gift of salvation, we not only escape punishment, we receive everlasting life in heaven.

Now, that's good news! And Edwards staked his life on

the goodness of God toward us. He wrote one of the most thorough bodies of theological work in America's history and distinguished himself as a great intellect of the early colonies. He also wrote about ethics, metaphysics, and psychology. After graduating from Yale in 1726, Edwards pastored a Congregational church in Northampton, Massachusetts, followed by several years as a minister to groups of American Indians and whites in Stockbridge. A few weeks before his death from a smallpox vaccination, he was named president of the College of New Jersey. It later became Princeton University.

It's been recorded that when Edwards preached, hulking men fell to the ground in repentance. Others claim he was the theologian of the First Great Awakening, as important as George Whitefield in fostering that life-shaking revival. Both descriptions indicate Edwards was filled with the Spirit's power and fervor to bring the spiritually wayward into God's kingdom. Yet he also preached about loving ourselves because we're loved by the Creator, the happiness inherent in holiness, and the satisfaction of knowing God intimately. His outlook wasn't all "fire and brimstone." Rather, it was faithful to the Bible and culturally relevant to his times.

As you read these thirty devotionals excerpted from Edwards' sermons and edited for readability, you may change your mind (as I did) about the great preacher's messages. I hope you'll discover his heart fixed not on our liability to God but on His redeeming love.

—*Judith Couchman*
November 1999

PART ONE

The Way to Redemption

I will sing of my Redeemer,
And His wondrous love to me;
On the cruel cross He suffered,
From the curse to set me free.

I will praise my dear Redeemer,
His triumphant pow'r I'll tell,
How the victory He giveth
Over sin, and death, and hell.

Sing, oh, sing of my Redeemer,
With His blood He purchased me,
On the cross He sealed my pardon,
Paid the debt and made me free.

"My Redeemer"
by P. P. Bliss and James McGranahan

JONATHAN EDWARDS' INSIGHT
Jesus Christ is the only One who can truly save our souls.

DAY 1

God's Glory, Our Redemption

THOUGHT FOR TODAY
God's grace, working in our lives, glorifies Him.

WISDOM FROM SCRIPTURE
For the message of the cross is foolishness to those who are perishing, but to us who are being saved it is the power of God.

For it is written: "I will destroy the wisdom of the wise; the intelligence of the intelligent I will frustrate."

Where is the wise man? Where is the scholar? Where is the philosopher of this age? Has not God made foolish the wisdom of the world?

For since in the wisdom of God the world through its wisdom did not know him, God was pleased through the foolishness of what was preached to save those who believe.

Jews demand miraculous signs and Greeks look for wisdom, but we preach Christ crucified: a stumbling block to Jews and foolishness to Gentiles, but to those whom God has called, both Jews and Greeks, Christ the power of God and the wisdom of God.

For the foolishness of God is wiser than man's wisdom, and the weakness of God is stronger than man's strength.

Brothers, think of what you were when you were called. Not many of you were wise by human standards; not many were influential; not many were of noble birth.

But God chose the foolish things of the world to shame the wise; God chose the weak things of the world to shame the strong.

He chose the lowly things of this world and the despised things—and the things that are not—to nullify the things that are, so that no one may boast before him.

It is because of him that you are in Christ Jesus, who has become for us wisdom from God—that is, our righteousness, holiness and redemption.

1 CORINTHIANS 1:18-30, NIV

INSIGHTS FROM JONATHAN EDWARDS

Those Christians to whom the apostle directed this epistle lived in a part of the world where human wisdom was exalted. Corinth was not far from Athens, which had been for many ages the most famous seat of philosophy and learning in the world. The apostle in response explains how God by the gospel destroyed and brought to nothing their wisdom.

The learned Grecians and their great philosophers by all their wisdom did not know God. They were not able to find out the truth in divine things. But after they had done their utmost to no effect, it pleased God to reveal Himself by the gospel, which they considered foolishness. And the apostle informs them in the text why God did this: that no flesh should glory in His presence.

All the good that we have is in and through Christ. He is wisdom, righteousness, sanctification, and redemption. Everything good in the fallen and redeemed creature is found in these four things. Christ is each of them to us, and we have none of them except through Him.

He is unto us wisdom: in Him is all the true excellency of understanding. Wisdom was a thing the Greeks admired, but Christ is the true Light of the world. It is through him alone that true wisdom is imparted to the mind.

It is in and through Christ that we have righteousness. It is by being in Him that we are justified, have our sins pardoned, and are received as righteous into God's favor.

It is through Christ that we have sanctification. We have in Him true excellency of heart as well as understanding, and He is made unto us inherent as well as imputed righteousness.

It is through Christ that we have redemption—the actual deliverance from all misery and the bestowment of all happiness and glory. Everything we have that is good comes through Christ, who is God.

It is God who has given us Christ, that we might have these benefits through Him. Through God, Christ is made unto us wisdom, righteousness, sanctification, and redemption. It is through God that we are in Christ Jesus, and come to Him, and so receive these blessings. It is God who gives us the faith whereby we know Christ.

Everything the redeemed have, we have by the grace of God. It was by grace that God gave us His only begotten Son. The gift was infinitely precious because Christ was infinitely worthy, a person of infinite glory, infinitely near and dear to God.

The grace is great in proportion to the benefit we have been given. The benefit is doubly infinite in that through Christ we have deliverance from an infinite, eternal misery and instead receive eternal joy and glory.

The grace of this gift is great, too, in proportion to our unworthiness. Instead of deserving such a gift, we merited infinite ill from God's hands.

The grace is great according to the manner in which it was given, and in proportion to the humiliation and expense of the method and means by which it was given. God gave Christ to dwell among us; He gave Him to us incarnate, in our own

nature. He gave him to us in a low and afflicted state, as slain, that He might be a feast for our souls.

—*God Glorified in Man's Dependence*

QUESTIONS TO CONSIDER
1. In what specific ways has God redeemed your life?
2. How do you need grace and redemption today?

A PRAYERFUL RESPONSE
Lord, thank You for Your gifts of grace and redemption. Amen.

Free Pardon for Sinners

THOUGHT FOR TODAY

God offers free pardon to those who seek His forgiveness.

WISDOM FROM SCRIPTURE

To You, O LORD, I lift up my soul; in You I trust, O my God. Do not let me be put to shame, nor let my enemies triumph over me.

No one whose hope is in You will ever be put to shame, but they will be put to shame who are treacherous without excuse.

Show me Your ways, O LORD, teach me Your paths; guide me in Your truth and teach me, for You are God my Savior, and my hope is in You all day long.

Remember, O LORD, Your great mercy and love, for they are from of old.

Remember not the sins of my youth and my rebellious ways; according to Your love remember me, for You are good, O LORD.

Good and upright is the LORD; therefore he instructs sinners in His ways.

He guides the humble in what is right and teaches them His way.

All the ways of the LORD are loving and faithful for those who keep the demands of His covenant.

For the sake of Your name, O LORD, forgive my iniquity, though it is great.

Who, then, is the man that fears the LORD? He will instruct him in the way chosen for him.

He will spend his days in prosperity, and his descendants will inherit the land.

The LORD confides in those who fear Him; He makes His covenant known to them.

My eyes are ever on the LORD, for only He will release my feet from the snare.

Turn to me and be gracious to me, for I am lonely and afflicted.

The troubles of my heart have multiplied; free me from my anguish.

Look upon my affliction and my distress and take away all my sins.

See how my enemies have increased and how fiercely they hate me!

Guard my life and rescue me; let me not be put to shame, for I take refuge in You.

May integrity and uprightness protect me, because my hope is in You.

Redeem Israel, O God, from all their troubles!

PSALM 25:1-22, NIV

INSIGHTS FROM JONATHAN EDWARDS

It is evident by some passages in this psalm that when it was penned, it was a time of affliction and danger for David. This appears particularly by the fifteenth and following verses: "Mine eyes are ever towards the Lord; for He shall pluck my feet out of the net." David's distress makes him think of his sins and leads him to confess them and to cry to God for pardon, as is suitable in a time of affliction. See verse 7: "Remember not the sins of my youth, nor my transgressions." And verse 18: "Look upon mine affliction, and my pain, and forgive all my sins."

The psalmist makes use of a specific argument in pleading for pardon. He pleads for pardon for God's name's sake. He has no expectation of pardon for the sake of any righteousness or worthiness for any good deeds he had done or any compensation he had made for his sins, though if a person's righteousness could be a just plea, David would have had as much to plead as most. But he begs that God would pardon him for His own name's sake, for His own glory, for the glory of His own free grace, and for the honor of His own covenant faithfulness.

The psalmist pleads the greatness of his sins as an argument for mercy. He could not plead his own righteousness or the smallness of his sins. He could not say, "Pardon mine iniquity, for I have done much good to counterbalance it." Or, "Pardon mine iniquity, for it is small, and You have no great reason to be angry with me. My iniquity is not so great that You have any just cause to remember it against me; my offence is such that You may well enough overlook it." But on the contrary he says, "Pardon mine iniquity, for it is great." He pleads the greatness of his sin and not the smallness of it. He enforces his prayer with this consideration: that his sins are very heinous.

But how could he make this a plea for pardon? Because the greater his iniquity was, the more he needed pardon. It is as if he had said, "Pardon mine iniquity, for it is so great that I cannot bear the punishment. My sin is so great that I am in need of pardon. My case will be exceedingly miserable unless You pardon me." He makes use of the greatness of his sin to enforce his plea for pardon, as a person would make use of the greatness of calamity in begging for relief.

When a beggar begs for bread, he will plead the greatness of his poverty and necessity. When a person in distress cries for pity, what more suitable plea can be urged than the extremity of his case? God allows such a plea as this. He is moved to mercy toward us not by anything in us but by the misery of our case. He does not pity sinners because they are worthy but because they need His pity.

The mercy of God is as sufficient for the pardon of the greatest sins as for the least, because His mercy is infinite. That which is infinite is as much above what is great as it is above what is small. Thus, God being infinitely great, He is as much above kings as He is above beggars; He is as much above the highest angel as He is above the meanest person. One finite measure does not come any nearer to what is infinite than another. Because the mercy of God is infinite, it is as sufficient for the pardon of all sin as of one.

Christ will not refuse to save the greatest sinners who come to God for mercy. This is Christ's work. It is His business to be a Savior of sinners. It is the work for which He came into the world; He will not object to it. He did not come to call the righteous but to call sinners to repentance. Sin is the very evil which He came into the world to remedy. Therefore He will not object to any person who is very sinful. The more sinful a person is, the more he needs Christ.

The sinfulness of humanity was the reason for Christ's coming into the world, the very misery from which He came to deliver men and women. The more misery they have, the more they need deliverance. The physician will not object to a person asking for healing if the person stands in great need of his help. If a physician of compassion comes among the sick and wounded, surely if he is able to, he will not refuse to heal those who stand most in need of healing.

The glory of grace by the redemption of Christ is sufficient for the pardon of the greatest sinners. The greatness of divine grace appears very much in this: that God through Christ saves the greatest offenders. The greater the guilt of any sinner, the more glorious and wonderful is the grace manifested in his pardon.

—*Pardon for the Greatest of Sinners*

QUESTIONS TO CONSIDER

1. Why would regular confession of sins be important?
2. How could regular confession change your life?

A PRAYERFUL RESPONSE

Lord, I ask for Your forgiveness today. Amen.

DAY 3

Sinners in God's Hands

THOUGHT FOR TODAY
God's love and mercy open the door to heaven.

WISDOM FROM SCRIPTURE
[Jesus said,] "There was a rich man who was dressed in purple and fine linen and lived in luxury every day.

"At his gate was laid a beggar named Lazarus, covered with sores and longing to eat what fell from the rich man's table. Even the dogs came and licked his sores.

"The time came when the beggar died and the angels carried him to Abraham's side. The rich man also died and was buried.

"In hell, where he was in torment, he looked up and saw Abraham far away, with Lazarus by his side.

"So he called to him, 'Father Abraham, have pity on me and send Lazarus to dip the tip of his finger in water and cool my tongue, because I am in agony in this fire.'

"But Abraham replied, 'Son, remember that in your lifetime you received your good things, while Lazarus received bad things, but now he is comforted here and you are in agony.

"And besides all this, between us and you a great chasm has been fixed, so that those who want to go from here to you cannot, nor can anyone cross over from there to us.'

"He answered, 'Then I beg you, father, send Lazarus to my father's house, for I have five brothers. Let him warn them, so that they will not also come to this place of torment.'

"Abraham replied, 'They have Moses and the Prophets; let them listen to them.'

"'No, father Abraham,' he said, 'but if someone from the dead goes to them, they will repent.'

"He said to him, 'If they do not listen to Moses and the Prophets, they will not be convinced even if someone rises from the dead.'"

Luke 16:19-31, NIV

INSIGHTS FROM JONATHAN EDWARDS

God has the power to cast the wicked into hell at any moment. Human hands cannot be strong when God rises up. The strongest people have no power to resist Him, nor can any escape His hands. He is able to cast the wicked into hell, and He can most easily do it.

Sometimes an earthly prince meets great difficulty in subduing a rebel who has found means to fortify himself and who has made himself strong by the numbers of his followers. But it is not so with God. There is no fortress that is any defense against the power of God.

Though hand join in hand and vast multitudes of God's enemies combine and associate themselves, they are easily broken into pieces. They are as great heaps of light chaff before the whirlwind or large quantities of dry stubble before devouring flames. We find it easy to crush a worm crawling on the earth or to cut or singe a slender thread by which an insect hangs. Likewise, it is easy for God, when He pleases, to cast His enemies down to hell. Who are we, that we should think to stand before Him at whose rebuke the earth trembles and the rocks are thrown down?

All the prudence and care people take to preserve themselves, or the care others take to preserve them, do not for a moment secure their lives. To this, divine providence and universal experience bear testimony: human wisdom is no security from death. If it were otherwise, we would see some difference with regard to a tendency toward early and unexpected death between the wise and politic of the world and others. But how is it in fact? Ecclesiastes 2:16 answers, "How dieth the wise man? Even as the fool."

God is under no obligation to keep any person out of hell. God certainly has made no promises either of eternal life or of any deliverance or preservation from eternal death, except for those contained in the covenant of grace. These promises are given in Christ, in whom all promises are yea and amen. But surely those who are not children of the covenant have no interest in the promises of the covenant of grace. They do not believe in any of the promises and have no interest in the Mediator of the covenant.

So it is plain and manifest that whatever pains a person takes in religion, whatever prayers he makes, till he believes in Christ, God is under no obligation to keep him a moment from eternal destruction.

And now you have an extraordinary opportunity, a day wherein Christ has thrown the door of mercy wide open and stands calling and crying with a loud voice to poor sinners. It is a day wherein many are flocking to Him and pressing into the kingdom of God. Many are daily coming from the east, west, north, and south. Many who were in the same miserable condition that you are in are now in a happy state, rejoicing in the hope of the glory of God, their hearts filled with love toward Him who has loved them and washed them from their sins in His own blood.

How awful to be left behind on such a day! To see so many others feasting, while you are pining and perishing! To see so many rejoicing and singing for joy of heart, while you have cause to mourn for sorrow of heart and howl for vexation of spirit! How can you rest one moment in such a condition? Are not your souls as precious as the souls of people who are flocking to Christ?

Therefore let everyone who is not of Christ now awake and fly from the wrath to come. Let everyone fly out of Sodom: "Haste and escape for your lives, look not behind you, escape to the mountain, lest you be consumed" (Genesis 19:17).

—*Sinners in the Hands of an Angry God*

QUESTIONS TO CONSIDER

1. Are you confident of your place in eternity?
2. What does God's covenant of grace mean to you?

A PRAYERFUL RESPONSE

Lord, help me to rest in Your covenant of grace through the shed blood of Christ. Amen.

DAY 4

A Time For Rejoicing

THOUGHT FOR TODAY
There will be a day when all that is wrong is made right.

WISDOM FROM SCRIPTURE
All the nations will be gathered before Him, and He will separate the people one from another as a shepherd separates the sheep from the goats.

He will put the sheep on His right and the goats on His left.

Then the King will say to those on His right, "Come, you who are blessed by My Father; take your inheritance, the kingdom prepared for you since the creation of the world.

"For I was hungry and you gave Me something to eat, I was thirsty and you gave Me something to drink, I was a stranger and you invited Me in, I needed clothes and you clothed Me, I was sick and you looked after Me, I was in prison and you came to visit Me."

Then the righteous will answer Him, "LORD, when did we see You hungry and feed You, or thirsty and give You something to drink?"

"When did we see You a stranger and invite You in, or needing clothes and clothed You?"

"When did we see You sick or in prison and go to visit You?"

The King will reply, "I tell you the truth, whatever you did for one of the least of these brothers of Mine, you did for Me."

Then He will say to those on His left, "Depart from Me, you who are cursed, into the eternal fire prepared for the devil and his angels."

MATTHEW 25:32-41, NIV

Not only will God's wrath be executed on the wicked; God will also destroy His enemies. For those who have been the enemies of God and Jesus Christ, whether or not they have been followers of the Antichrist does not alter the case. The wicked will be destroyed together, as if united in the same cause and interest, as if all soldiers of Satan's army. They will all stand together at the day of judgment as belonging to the same company.

At the day of judgment the saints in glory at Christ's right hand will see the wicked at His left hand, confused and horrified as they hear the judge pronounce sentence upon them: "Depart, ye cursed, into everlasting fire, prepared for the devil and his angels." The saints will see the wicked go away into everlasting punishment.

As well, the Scripture seems to indicate that not only will the saints apprehend the misery of the wicked, but the damned in hell will also apprehend the happiness of the heavenly inhabitants. The two worlds of happiness and misery will be in view of each other. The saints in glory will see how the damned are tormented; they will see God's warnings fulfilled and His wrath executed upon sinners. And they will rejoice, because in God's wrath they will see His glory.

The glory of God appears in all His works; therefore this work of God which the saints in glory behold will be an occasion for rejoicing. God glorifies Himself in all that He does, but He glorifies Himself principally in the eternal disposal of His intelligent creatures, some appointed to everlasting life and others left to everlasting death. And so God glorifies Himself in the eternal damnation of the ungodly.

The saints in heaven will be perfect in their love for God. Their hearts will be a flame of love to God, and they will greatly value the glory of God. Those who know Him already highly value the glory of God on earth; how much more will they value it in the world to come! They will exceedingly delight in seeing God glorified. They will greatly rejoice in all that contributes to His glory.

The glory of God will in their esteem be of greater consequence than the welfare of thousands and millions of souls. Particularly, the saints will rejoice in seeing the justice of God glorified in the sufferings of the damned. The misery of the damned, dreadful as it is, is only what justice requires.

Those in heaven will see and know this much more clearly than any of us do here. They will see how perfectly just and righteous the punishment of the wicked is, and therefore how properly inflicted by the supreme Governor of the world. They will greatly rejoice to see justice take place, to see that all the sin and wickedness that has been committed in the world is remembered by God and has its due punishment. The sight of this strict and immutable justice of God will render Him amiable and adorable in their eyes. The saints in heaven will rejoice when they see God their Father so glorious in His justice.

Then there will be no remaining difficulties about the justice of God, about the absolute decrees of God, or about anything else pertaining to the dispensations of God toward humanity. Divine justice in the destruction of the wicked will appear as light without darkness and will shine as the sun without clouds. On this account will we sing joyful songs of praise to God, as the saints and angels do when He pours the vials of His wrath upon the Antichrist (Revelation 16:1). Indeed, they sing joyfully to God on this account: that His judgments are true and righteous (16:7).

Seeing God's justice will cause the saints to value His love the more, and His mercy and grace as well. The more we apprehend God's justice, the more we will prize and rejoice in His love.

—The End of the Wicked Contemplated by the Righteous

QUESTIONS TO CONSIDER
1. How do you feel when you see injustice? Why?
2. How do you feel about God justifying all things in the end?

A PRAYERFUL RESPONSE
Lord, teach me to wait patiently for Your final justice. Amen.

DAY 5

Redeeming the Soul

THOUGHT FOR TODAY
There is no price too high to pay for a soul.

WISDOM FROM SCRIPTURE
But even if you should suffer for what is right, you are blessed. "Do not fear what they fear; do not be frightened."

But in your hearts set apart Christ as Lord. Always be prepared to give an answer to everyone who asks you to give the reason for the hope that you have. But do this with gentleness and respect, keeping a clear conscience, so that those who speak maliciously against your good behavior in Christ may be ashamed of their slander.

It is better, if it is God's will, to suffer for doing good than for doing evil.

For Christ died for sins once for all, the righteous for the unrighteous, to bring you to God. He was put to death in the body but made alive by the Spirit, through whom also He went and preached to the spirits in prison who disobeyed long ago when God waited patiently in the days of Noah while the ark was being built. In it only a few people, eight in all, were saved through water, and this water symbolizes baptism that now saves you also—not the removal of dirt from the body but the pledge of a good conscience toward God. It saves you by the resurrection of Jesus Christ, who has gone into heaven and is at God's right hand—with angels, authorities and powers in submission to Him.

1 PETER 3:14-22, NIV

Building the ark was a great undertaking, assigned to Noah that he and his family might be saved. The ark was a building of vast size; the length of it was three hundred cubits, the breadth of it fifty cubits, and the height of it thirty cubits.

It was a lengthy undertaking to build a structure with all those apartments and divisions in it, and capable of floating upon water for an extended time. It took Noah, with all the workmen he employed, 120 years or thereabouts to build it. God had before this time warned His people, "My Spirit shall not always strive with man" (Genesis 6:3), but during those 120 years "the long-suffering of God" waited on the world (1 Peter 3:20) and the Spirit of God did strive with humans.

People would hold in high esteem an undertaking that would keep them employed for even half the time that Noah employed himself in this business of building the ark. He must have had a great and constant care upon his mind for those 120 years, superintending the work and seeing that all was done exactly according to the directions that God had given him.

For not only was Noah himself continually employed in the undertaking, but also a great number of workmen were constantly procuring, collecting, and fitting materials and putting them together. How great a thing it was for Noah to undertake such a work!

Besides the continual care and labor, the work was of vast expense. Probably not one of that wicked generation lifted a finger to help Noah, doubtless believing the work was the fruit of his own folly.

Noah must have been very rich to bear the expense of such a work and to pay so many workmen for so long a time. It would have been a great expense for a prince, and doubtless Noah was very rich, as Abraham and Job were afterward. But probably Noah spent all his worldly substance in this work, thus manifesting his faith in the word of God. He sold all that he had, believing there would surely come a flood which would destroy everything. If he kept what he had, it would be of no service to him. Herein he set an example for us, showing us how we ought to sell all we have for our salvation.

Noah's undertaking was of great difficulty because it exposed him to the continual reproaches of his neighbors for that whole 120 years. None of them believed what he said about a flood that would drown the world. To undertake such a vast piece of work—under the notion that it would be his means of salvation when the world was destroyed—made him the continual laughingstock of the world. When he was about to hire workmen, doubtless everyone laughed at him. We may suppose that though the workmen consented to work for wages, they laughed at the folly of their employer. When the ark was being built, we may suppose that everyone who passed by laughed at it, calling it Noah's folly.

In these days people are reluctant to submit to something that makes them objects of reproach or ridicule. If, however, while some are reproaching a person others stand by and honor him, he may be sustained. But still it is difficult for someone to make himself the laughingstock of the whole world, despised by all.

Where is the person who can stand the shock of such a trial for even twenty years? Yet Noah, at the divine direction, engaged and went through it for 120 years so he and his family might be saved from the destruction that was to visit the world. "According to all that God commanded him, so did he" (Genesis 6:22).

Time did not weary Noah. He did not grow weary of his vast expense. He stood the shock of his neighbors' derision and the ridicule of all the world year after year. He did not grow weary of being their laughingstock, so as to give up his enterprise; he persevered in it till the ark was finished. And after this, he had the trouble and charge of procuring goods for the maintenance of his family, and of all the various kinds of creatures, for so long a time as they were to be afloat.

Noah engaged in his undertaking to gain a temporal salvation. How great an undertaking then should we be willing to endure to inherit eternal salvation! A salvation from an eternal deluge, from being overwhelmed with the billows of God's wrath—of which Noah's flood was but a shadow.

—The Manner in Which the Salvation
of the Soul Is to Be Sought

QUESTIONS TO CONSIDER

1. How is today's society like that in Noah's time?
2. How might God be asking you to "pay the price" for the salvation of souls?

A PRAYERFUL RESPONSE

Lord, thank You for paying with Your life to redeem my soul. Amen.

DAY 6

Christ's Agony, Our Salvation

THOUGHT FOR TODAY
Through Christ's suffering, we have
received eternal life with God.

WISDOM FROM SCRIPTURE
Who has believed our message and to whom has the arm of the
LORD been revealed?

He grew up before Him like a tender shoot, and like a root
out of dry ground. He had no beauty or majesty to attract us to
Him, nothing in His appearance that we should desire Him.

He was despised and rejected by men, a man of sorrows, and
familiar with suffering. Like one from whom men hide their
faces He was despised, and we esteemed him not.

Surely He took up our infirmities and carried our sorrows,
yet we considered Him stricken by God, smitten by Him, and
afflicted.

But He was pierced for our transgressions, He was crushed
for our iniquities; the punishment that brought us peace was
upon Him, and by His wounds we are healed.

We all, like sheep, have gone astray, each of us has turned to his
own way; and the LORD has laid on Him the iniquity of us all.

He was oppressed and afflicted, yet He did not open his
mouth; He was led like a lamb to the slaughter, and as a sheep
before her shearers is silent, so He did not open his mouth.

By oppression and judgment He was taken away. And who
can speak of His descendants? For He was cut off from the land
of the living; for the transgression of my people he was stricken.

He was assigned a grave with the wicked, and with the rich in His death, though He had done no violence, nor was any deceit in His mouth.

Yet it was the LORD's will to crush Him and cause Him to suffer, and though the LORD makes His life a guilt offering, he will see His offspring and prolong His days, and the will of the LORD will prosper in His hand.

After the suffering of His soul, He will see the light and be satisfied; by His knowledge my righteous servant will justify many, and He will bear their iniquities.

ISAIAH 53:1-11, NIV

INSIGHTS FROM JONATHAN EDWARDS

Our Lord Jesus Christ, in His original nature, was infinitely above all suffering. He was God over all, blessed forevermore. But when He became a man, He was not only capable of suffering, He partook of that nature which is remarkably feeble and exposed to suffering.

Human nature, on account of its weakness, is in Scripture compared to the grass of the field, which easily withers and decays. It is compared to a leaf and to the dry stubble and to a blast of wind. The nature of feeble humanity is said to be only dust and ashes, to have its foundation in the dust, to be crushed before the moth. It was this nature, with all its weakness and exposure to sufferings, that Christ, who is God omnipotent, took upon Himself.

Neither did the Lord take human nature on Himself in its first, most perfect, and vigorous state, but in that feeble, forlorn state that is its character since the Fall. Therefore Christ is called "a tender plant" and "a root out of a dry ground." "For He shall grow up before Him as a tender plant, and as a root out of a dry ground: He hath no form nor comeliness; and when we shall see Him, there is no beauty that we should desire Him" (Isaiah 53:2).

Because Christ's principal errand in the world was suffering, He came with a nature and in such circumstances that made way for His suffering. His whole life was filled up with suffering. He began to suffer in His infancy, but His suffering increased the more He drew near to the close of His life. His suffering after His public ministry began was probably much greater than before, and the latter part of His public ministry seems to have been distinguished by suffering.

The longer Christ lived in the world—the more that people saw and heard of Him—the more they hated Him. His enemies were more and more enraged by His opposition to their lusts. The devil, having been often baffled by Him, grew more and more enraged and strengthened the battle more and more against Him. Consequently, the cloud over Christ's head grew darker and darker the longer He lived in the world, reaching its greatest blackness when He hung upon the cross and cried out, "My God, my God, why hast Thou forsaken me?"

We learn how dreadful Christ's last sufferings were from the effect that His foreknowledge of those sufferings had on Him. In the week before His death, His understanding of the sufferings to come was so dreadful that the very idea of them sank His soul down into the dark shadow of death. He actually sweat blood. His body was covered with clotted blood, and not only His body, but the very ground under Him. The blood had been forced through His pores by the violence of his agony.

And if only the foresight of the cup was so dreadful, how dreadful must have been the cup itself—how far beyond all that can be uttered or conceived!

Many of the martyrs have endured extreme tortures, but from what we read in Scripture there is reason to believe those tortures were nothing compared to the last sufferings of Christ on the cross. And what He endured in His body on the cross, though it was dreadful, was yet the least part of His sufferings, for He endured vastly greater torments in His soul.

Many of the martyrs have endured physical tortures as severe as Christ's. Many of the martyrs have been crucified in the manner Christ was. And yet their souls have not been overwhelmed in the manner Christ's soul was overwhelmed. No martyrs have suffered such amazing sorrow and distress of mind, either at the anticipation of their sufferings or in the actual endurance of them, as to sweat blood.

From what we know of Christ, we may see the wonderful strength of His love for sinners—a love so strong it carried Him through that agony. The love of any mere person or angel would doubtless have sunk under such a weight, and would never have endured an anguish of soul so strong as to cause a bloody sweat like that of Jesus Christ.

But His love for His enemies, poor and unworthy as they were, was stronger still. The heart of Christ was full of distress, but it was fuller of love for the wicked. His sorrows abounded, but His love did much more abound. Christ's soul was overwhelmed with a deluge of grief, but it poured from a deluge of love to sinners—a love sufficient to overflow the world and overwhelm the highest mountains of its sins. Those great drops of blood were a manifestation of an ocean of love in Christ's heart.

—*Christ's Agony*

QUESTIONS TO CONSIDER

1. How might you better understand all that Christ has suffered for you?
2. How could this understanding affect your relationship with Him?

A PRAYERFUL RESPONSE

Lord, help me to more fully appreciate Your suffering for me. Amen.

DAY 7

A Divine and Supernatural Light

THOUGHT FOR TODAY

As we walk in God's light, we see who we really are.

WISDOM FROM SCRIPTURE

This is the message we have heard from Him and declare to you: God is light; in Him there is no darkness at all.

If we claim to have fellowship with Him yet walk in the darkness, we lie and do not live by the truth.

But if we walk in the light, as He is in the light, we have fellowship with one another, and the blood of Jesus, his Son, purifies us from all sin.

If we claim to be without sin, we deceive ourselves and the truth is not in us.

If we confess our sins, He is faithful and just and will forgive us our sins and purify us from all unrighteousness.

If we claim we have not sinned, we make Him out to be a liar and His word has no place in our lives.

1 JOHN 1:5-10, NIV

INSIGHTS FROM JONATHAN EDWARDS

There is such a thing as a spiritual and divine light immediately imparted to the soul by God. It is of a different nature from any light that is obtained by natural means.

This spiritual and divine light is not merely those convictions that humans may have of their sin. People in their natural condition may have convictions of the guilt that lies upon them, of the anger of God, and of their danger of divine vengeance. Such convictions are from a light or sensibility of truth. That some sinners have a greater conviction of their guilt and misery than others is because some have more light—that is, a greater apprehension of truth—than others.

This light and conviction may well be from the Spirit of God. The Spirit may convince us of sin, yet in the convincing, nature may be much more at work than is divine light. In such cases the Spirit of God, rather than infusing any new principles, uses natural principles. Common grace differs from special grace in that it influences us by assisting nature, not by imparting grace or bestowing anything beyond nature.

This light is wholly natural, of no superiority to what mere nature provides, though it is more than people would obtain if left wholly to themselves. In other words, common grace assists the faculties of the soul only to do more fully that which they do by nature. Natural conscience or reason will, by mere nature, make a person sensible of guilt and will accuse and condemn him when he has done amiss. Conscience is a principle natural to humans. The work that it does naturally, of itself, is to give an apprehension of right and wrong. It suggests to the mind the relationship between right and wrong as well as retribution to come.

The Spirit of God, in those convictions which the unregenerate sometimes have, assists the conscience to do this work more fully than if people were left to themselves. He helps the conscience to stand against those things that tend to stupefy it and obstruct its exercise.

But in the renewing and sanctifying work of the Holy Ghost, those things are wrought in the soul that go beyond nature—things that by nature alone could not be wrought. With the Spirit of God at work, the mind may habitually exercise behavior that, under the dominion of sin, it had been incapable of—in the same way that a dead body is incapable of vital acts.

The Spirit of God acts in a different manner in the one case than in the other. He may indeed act *upon* the mind of a natural person, but He acts *within* the mind of a saint, as an indwelling, vital principle. He acts upon the minds of unregenerate persons as an extrinsic, occasional agent. But in acting upon them, He does not unite Himself with them. Despite all His influences, such persons are still sensual, having not the Spirit (Jude 19). But when He takes a saint for His temple, He does unite Himself with the mind of that saint, and begins to influence him as a new, supernatural principle of life and action.

The Spirit of God, acting in the soul of a godly person, exerts and communicates Himself there in His own proper nature. Holiness is the proper nature of the Spirit of God. The Holy Spirit operates in the minds of the godly by uniting Himself with them, living in them, and exerting His own nature in the exercise of their faculties.

The Spirit of God may act upon a creature, and yet in acting not communicate Himself. The Spirit of God may act upon inanimate objects, as He moved upon the face of the waters at the beginning of creation. So the Spirit of God may act upon the human mind in many ways and communicate Himself no more than when He acts upon an inanimate object. For instance, He may excite thoughts in persons, assist their natural reason and understanding, or assist other natural principles— but without any union with their souls. He may act as if upon an external object.

But when the Spirit enacts His holy influences and spiritual operations, He peculiarly communicates Himself in such a way that the subject is spiritually dominated. It may be thus described: a true sense of the divine excellency of the things revealed in the Word of God, as well as a conviction of the truth and reality of those things, arise within the person. This conviction is a natural consequence of seeing their divine glory.

—A Divine and Supernatural Light

QUESTIONS TO CONSIDER
1. How does God's light affect your life?
2. What has God revealed to you in His Word today?

A PRAYERFUL RESPONSE
Lord, shine Your light through the darkness in my life. Amen.

The Mercy of God

THOUGHT FOR TODAY

God is just in punishment, but merciful in pardon.

WISDOM FROM SCRIPTURE

Does God pervert justice? Does the Almighty pervert what is right?

When your children sinned against Him, He gave them over to the penalty of their sin.

But if you will look to God and plead with the Almighty, if you are pure and upright, even now He will rouse Himself on your behalf and restore you to your rightful place.

Your beginnings will seem humble, so prosperous will your future be.

Ask the former generations and find out what their fathers learned, for we were born only yesterday and know nothing, and our days on earth are but a shadow.

Will they not instruct you and tell you? Will they not bring forth words from their understanding?

Can papyrus grow tall where there is no marsh? Can reeds thrive without water?

While still growing and uncut, they wither more quickly than grass.

Such is the destiny of all who forget God; so perishes the hope of the godless.

JOB 8:3-13, NIV

Every crime or fault deserves a greater or lesser punishment, in proportion to the crime. If any fault deserves punishment, then the greater the fault, the greater the punishment. If there be any such thing as a fault infinitely heinous, it will follow that it is just to inflict a punishment for it that is infinitely dreadful.

In turn, our obligation to love, honor, and obey any person is in proportion to that person's loveliness, honorableness, and authority, for that is the very meaning of the words. When we say someone is very lovely, it is the same as saying he is one very much to be loved. Or if we say someone is more honorable than another, the meaning of the words is that he is one whom we are more obliged to honor. If we say anyone has great authority over us, it is the same as saying he has a great right to our subjection and obedience.

God is a being infinitely lovely because He has infinite excellency and beauty. To have infinite excellency and beauty is the same as to have infinite loveliness. He is a being of infinite greatness, majesty, and glory; therefore He is infinitely honorable. He is infinitely exalted above the greatest potentates of the earth and the highest angels in heaven, and therefore He is infinitely more honorable than they. His authority over us is infinite, and His right to our obedience is infinitely strong. He is infinitely worthy to be obeyed, and we have an absolute, universal, and infinite dependence on Him.

If there be any evil in sin against God, it must be infinite evil. Be it ever so small upon other accounts, it still has one infinite dimension: it has an infinite aggravation, for it is a sin against an infinite being. And so it is an infinite evil.

Human nature teaches us that when an injury is voluntary, it is faulty, without any consideration of what might have caused the evil act of the will. People will mention others' corrupt nature, when they are injured, as a thing that aggravates their crime— even when they also are at fault.

How common it is for a person, when he perceives himself greatly injured by another, to complain against him and point out his baseness. He might say, "He is a man of a most perverse spirit; he is naturally of a selfish or proud and haughty temper. He has a base and vile disposition." And yet with respect to their sins against God, people's natural and corrupt dispositions are mentioned as an excuse for them, as if such excuses rendered them blameless.

But herein we can comprehend the justice of God. If people were guilty of only one sin, that sin is sufficient ground for their rejection and condemnation. If they are sinners, that is enough. No matter how small, any fault is sufficient to keep them from ever lifting their heads and to cause them to cry with the publican, "God, be merciful to me, a sinner!"

But sinful people are full of sin, full of principles and acts of sin. Their guilt is like great mountains heaped one upon another, till the pile reaches up to heaven. They are totally corrupt in every part: in all their faculties; in all the principles of their nature, understandings, and wills; and in all their dispositions and affections. Their heads and their hearts are totally depraved. All the members of their bodies are instruments of sin. All their senses—seeing, hearing, tasting—are only inlets and outlets of sin. There is nothing but sin, no good at all.

In this world there are wickednesses without number or measure. There are breaches of every command in thought, word, and deed. There are lives full of sin, days and nights filled up with sin. There are mercies abused and frowns despised, mercy and justice and all the divine perfections trampled on. The honor of each person in the Trinity is trod in the dirt. Now if a single sinful word or thought has so much evil in it as to deserve eternal destruction, how do they who are guilty of so much sin deserve to be eternally cast off and destroyed!

I would conclude this discourse by putting the godly in mind of the freeness and wonderfulness of the grace of God toward them. Your case is no different than what you have heard: you, also, had a wicked heart; you, also, lived a wicked life; and it would have been just for God to cast you off forever. But He has had mercy upon you; He has made His glorious grace appear in your everlasting salvation.

God not only continued those mercies, He bestowed unspeakably greater mercies upon you. You refused to hear when God called, yet God heard you when you called. You abused God's infinite mercy to encourage yourself in sin against Him, yet God has manifested that infinite mercy toward you. You have rejected Christ and set Him at naught, and yet He is become your Savior. You have neglected your own salvation, but God has not neglected it. You have destroyed yourself, but still God has been your help. God has magnified His free grace toward you and not to others because He has chosen you, and it has pleased Him to set His love upon you.

—*The Justice of God in the Damnation of Sinners*

QUESTIONS TO CONSIDER

1. What is the difference between actual acts of sin and a sin nature?

2. Why is all sin really rebellion against God rather than merely against people?

A PRAYERFUL RESPONSE

Lord, may I walk upright in Your eyes today. Amen.

DAY 9

Be Still and Know

THOUGHT FOR TODAY
God's greatness causes us to be still before Him.

WISDOM FROM SCRIPTURE

God is our refuge and strength, an ever-present help in trouble.

Therefore we will not fear, though the earth give way and the mountains fall into the heart of the sea, though its waters roar and foam and the mountains quake with their surging. *Selah.*

There is a river whose streams make glad the city of God, the holy place where the Most High dwells.

God is within her, she will not fall; God will help her at break of day.

Nations are in uproar, kingdoms fall; He lifts His voice, the earth melts.

The LORD Almighty is with us; the God of Jacob is our fortress. *Selah.*

Come and see the works of the LORD, the desolations He has brought on the earth.

He makes wars cease to the ends of the earth; He breaks the bow and shatters the spear, He burns the shields with fire.

"Be still, and know that I am God; I will be exalted among the nations, I will be exalted in the earth."

The LORD Almighty is with us; the God of Jacob is our fortress. *Selah.*

PSALM 46:1-11, NIV

To be still before God implies that we must be silent before Him. It means not speaking against the sovereign dispensations of Providence; not complaining about them; not darkening our counsel with words spoken without knowledge; not justifying ourselves; not speaking great, swelling words of vanity.

We must also be still as to our actions and outward behavior, so as not to oppose God in His dispensations. The inward frame of our hearts should be cultivating a calm and quiet submission of soul to the sovereign pleasure of God, whatever that might be.

We observe this duty because of the divinity of God. The fact that He is God is a sufficient reason why we should be still before Him, in no wise murmuring, objecting, or opposing, but instead calmly and humbly submitting to Him.

Our submission is to be such as becomes rational creatures. God could not require us to submit to Him contrary to reason, but to submit to Him because we understand the reason for so doing. In truth, the bare consideration that God is God may well be sufficient to still all objections and opposition against His divine and sovereign dispensations.

In that God is God, He is an absolutely and infinitely perfect being, and it is impossible that He should do amiss. As He is eternal and does not receive His existence from any other, He cannot be limited in His being or in any of His attributes to any certain, determinate quantity.

If anything has bounds fixed to it, there must be some cause or reason why those bounds are fixed just where they are. It follows, then, that every limited thing must have some cause, and that a being which has no cause must be unlimited.

It is evident by the works of God that His understanding and power are infinite. He who has made all things out of nothing and upholds, governs, and manages all things—every moment, in all ages, without growing weary—must be of infinite power. He must also be of infinite knowledge. If He made all things and upholds and governs all things continually, He then knows and perfectly sees all things, great and small, in heaven and earth, with infinite understanding.

Being thus infinite in understanding and power, He must also be perfectly holy, for unholiness always implies some defect, some blindness. Where there is no darkness or delusion, there can be no unholiness. It is impossible for wickedness to exist with infinite light. As God is infinite in power and knowledge, He must be self-sufficient and all-sufficient. Therefore it is impossible that He should be under any temptation to do anything amiss, for He can have no selfish end in doing it. When any are tempted to do amiss, it is for selfish ends. But how can an all-sufficient being who wants nothing be tempted to do evil for selfish ends? God is holy, and nothing is more impossible than that God should do amiss.

As He is God, He is so great that He is infinitely above all comprehension. Therefore it is unreasonable to quarrel with His dispensations. If He were a being whom we could comprehend, He would not be God. His dispensations are mysterious, and there are many other things in the nature of God and in His works and government that are mysterious to us, and which we never can fully find out.

What are we? And what do we make of ourselves when we expect that God and His ways should be upon a level with our own understandings? We are infinitely unequal to any such thing as comprehending God. What are we but babes? In truth, in comparison with the wisdom of God, our understandings are infinitely less than those of babes. It becomes us therefore to be sensible of our place and to behave ourselves accordingly.

This consideration alone, of the infinite distance between God and us and between God's understanding and ours, should be enough to still and quiet us concerning all that God does—however mysterious and unintelligible to our understanding.

—The Sole Consideration, That God Is God,
Sufficient to Still All Objections to His Sovereignty

QUESTIONS TO CONSIDER

1. Why can "being still" before God be difficult?
2. How can you learn to accept the mysteries of God?

A PRAYERFUL RESPONSE

Lord, teach me to be still in Your presence. Amen.

DAY 10

Seeking the Kingdom of God

THOUGHT FOR TODAY
We are called to focus our lives on Christ and His kingdom.

WISDOM FROM SCRIPTURE
As Jesus and His disciples were on their way, He came to a village where a woman named Martha opened her home to Him.

She had a sister called Mary, who sat at the Lord's feet listening to what He said.

But Martha was distracted by all the preparations that had to be made. She came to him and asked, "Lord, don't you care that my sister has left me to do the work by myself? Tell her to help me!"

"Martha, Martha," the Lord answered, "you are worried and upset about many things, but only one thing is needed. Mary has chosen what is better, and it will not be taken away from her."

LUKE 10:38-42, NIV

"The kingdom of heaven is like treasure hidden in a field. When a man found it, he hid it again, and then in his joy went and sold all he had and bought that field.

"Again, the kingdom of heaven is like a merchant looking for fine pearls.

"When he found one of great value, he went away and sold everything he had and bought it."

MATTHEW 13:44-46, NIV

In general, people who live under the light of the gospel, and who are not atheists, desire the kingdom of God. That is, they desire to go to heaven rather than to hell. However, most of them are not much concerned about it; on the contrary, they live a secure and careless life.

Some people under the awakening of God's Spirit are many degrees above these, yet they are still not seeking the kingdom of God. But others do have strong desires to get out of their natural condition and to follow Christ. They are so convicted of the misery of their present state, and of the extreme necessity of obtaining a better life, that their minds are wrapped up in concern about it.

These people desire salvation above all things in the world. This concern is so great that it shuts out other concerns. They used to desire other things, or at least had their concern divided between God and other things. But when it comes to seeking the kingdom of God, this concern prevails above all others. It lays other things low; it engrosses the mind.

Not only should the search for eternal life be the one concern on which our souls focus, but salvation should be sought as the one thing needful (Luke 10:42) and the one thing desired (Psalm 27:4). Seeking the kingdom of heaven denotes an earnestness and firmness of resolution. There should be a strength of resolution accompanying the strength of desire. Besides desiring salvation, we should earnestly resolve to pursue it as much as lies in our power. We are to do all that we are able to do, resisting and fighting against all manner of sin, to continue in such a pursuit.

There are two things needful in a person as he pursues these resolutions. There must be a sense of the great importance of the mercy sought, and there must also be a sense of opportunity to obtain it.

The strength of resolution depends on the sense of these things that God gives to the heart. Persons without such a sense may seem to themselves to take up resolutions; they may force a promise to themselves and say, "I will seek as long as I live; I will not give up till I obtain." But they deceive themselves. Their hearts are not in it; neither do they truly resolve to pursue salvation. They make a resolution of the mouth more than of the heart; their hearts are not strongly bent to fulfill what their mouth says.

The firmness of the resolution lies in the disposition of the heart. Those who are seeking the kingdom of God have a disposition of heart to do everything that is required and lies in their power to do, and to continue in their resolve. They have not only earnestness, but steadiness of resolution. They do not seek with a wavering, unsteady heart. The constant bent of the soul is to obtain the kingdom of God.

Where there is strength of desire and firmness of resolution, there will be answerable endeavors. Persons thus engaged in their hearts will strive to enter in at the straight gate and will be violent for heaven. Their practice will be agreeable to the counsel of the wise man in Proverbs 2:1-5: "My son, if thou wilt receive my words, and hide my commandments with thee; so that thou incline thine ear unto wisdom, and apply thine heart to understanding; yea, if thou criest after knowledge, and liftest up thy voice for understanding; if thou seekest her as silver, and searchest for her as for hidden treasures; then shalt thou understand the fear of the LORD, and find the knowledge of God."

Here, earnest desire and strong resolution are signified by

inclining the ear to wisdom and applying the heart to understanding. Great endeavor is denoted by crying after knowledge and lifting up the voice for understanding, seeking her as silver and searching for her as for hidden treasures. Such desires and resolutions and such endeavors go together. Seeking the kingdom of God denotes an engagedness and earnestness that is directly about the business of getting into the kingdom of God.

—*Pressing Into the Kingdom of God*

QUESTIONS TO CONSIDER

1. Even if you have already received salvation, how could you still actively seek the kingdom of God?
2. Whom might you help to enter into God's kingdom? How?

A PRAYERFUL RESPONSE

Lord, I want to bring others into Your kingdom. Amen.

The Sweetness of Christ

THOUGHT FOR TODAY
The kindness of Christ leads us to repentance.

WISDOM FROM SCRIPTURE

No one who denies the Son has the Father; whoever acknowledges the Son has the Father also.

See that what you have heard from the beginning remains in you. If it does, you also will remain in the Son and in the Father.

And this is what He promised us—even eternal life.

I am writing these things to you about those who are trying to lead you astray.

As for you, the anointing you received from Him remains in you, and you do not need anyone to teach you. But as His anointing teaches you about all things and as that anointing is real, not counterfeit—just as it has taught you, remain in Him.

And now, dear children, continue in Him, so that when He appears we may be confident and unashamed before Him at his coming.

If you know that He is righteous, you know that everyone who does what is right has been born of Him.

How great is the love the Father has lavished on us, that we should be called children of God! And that is what we are! The reason the world does not know us is that it did not know Him.

1 JOHN 2:23-3:1, NIV

Christ, in his love, compassion, and graciousness, is inclined to receive all who come to Him. If He did not, He would fail in His own undertaking, and also in His promise both to the Father and to us. His wisdom and faithfulness will not allow that. He is full of love and kindness and, if we come to Him, disposed to receive and defend us.

Christ is exceedingly ready to pity us; His arms are open to receive us. He delights to receive and protect distressed souls who come to Him. He desires to gather them as a hen gathers her chickens under her wings. It is a work He exceedingly rejoices in, because He delights in acts of love, pity, and mercy.

How happy would you be if only your hearts were persuaded to cling to Jesus Christ! Then you would be out of danger: whatever storms and tempests were without, you might rest securely within. You might hear the rushing of the wind and the thunder roaring abroad, while you were safe in this hiding place.

Oh, be persuaded to hide yourself in Christ Jesus! What greater assurance of safety can you desire? He has undertaken to defend and save you, if you will come to Him. He looks upon it as His work. He engaged in it before the world was, and He has given His faithful promise, which He will not break. If only you will make your flight to Him, His life shall be laid down for yours. He will answer for you, and you shall have nothing to do but rest quietly in Him. You may stand still and see what the Lord will do for you. If there be anything to suffer, the suffering is Christ's. You will have nothing to suffer. If there be anything to be done, the doing of it is Christ's. You will have nothing to do but to stand still and behold it.

You will certainly be accepted of the Father if your soul lays hold of Jesus Christ. Christ is chosen and anointed of the Father and sent forth to save those in danger and fear. He is greatly beloved of God, even infinitely, and God will accept those who are in Christ. If you are in Christ, justice and the law will not be against you. That threatening verse, "in the day that thou eatest thou shalt die" (Genesis 2:17), in its proper sense, will not touch you.

The majesty and honor of God are not against you. You need not be afraid that you shall not be justified if you come to Him. There is an act of justification already past and declared for all who come to God by the resurrection of Christ, and as soon as ever you come you are declared free. If you come to Christ, it will be a sure sign that He loved you from all eternity past and that He died for you. And you may be sure that if He died for you, He had reason to: that is, that He is committed to the dispensation of life.

Let this truth cause believers to prize the Lord Jesus Christ even more. Consider that it is He and He alone who defends you from wrath; consider, moreover, that He is a safe defense. Your defense is a high tower; your city of refuge is impregnable. There is no rock like your rock. There is none like Christ, "the God of Jeshurun, who rideth upon the heaven in thy help, and in His excellency on the sky; the eternal God is thy refuge, and underneath are everlasting arms" (Deuteronomy 33:26-27).

He in whom you trust is a buckler to all that trust in Him. Prize that Savior, who keeps your soul in safety while thousands of others are carried away by the fury of God's anger and are tossed with raging and burning tempests into hell! How much better is your case than theirs! And to whom is it owing but to the Lord Jesus Christ? Remember what was once your case, and what it is now, and prize Jesus Christ.

Let those Christians who have doubts and fears concerning their condition fly often to Jesus Christ, who is a hiding place from the wind and a covering from the tempest. Most Christians are at times afraid they will miscarry their faith at the last. The best remedy for them is the soul's resort to this hiding place. The same act which at first gave comfort and peace will give peace again. They who clearly see the sufficiency of Christ and the safety of committing themselves to Him to save them from what they fear will rest in the knowledge that He will defend them.

Be directed therefore at such times to do as the psalmist did in Psalm 56:3-4: "What time I am afraid, I will trust in Thee. In God I will praise His word; in God I have put my trust: I will not fear what flesh can do unto me."

It is said that because there is such a fullness in Him, so plentiful a provision for the satisfaction of the needy and longing soul, Christ is a river of water. When one is extremely thirsty, a small draught of water will not satisfy him; but when he comes to a river he finds a fullness, and there he may drink full draughts. Christ is like a river in that He has a sufficiency not only for one thirsty soul but for many. In supplying one soul with water the fountain is not lessened, so that those who come afterward must go without. A thirsty person does not lessen a river by quenching his thirst.

Christ is like a river in another respect. A river is continually flowing; there are fresh supplies of water coming from the fountainhead continually, so that a person may live by it and be supplied with water all his life. So Christ is an ever-flowing fountain. He is continually supplying his people, yet the fountain is never spent. They who live upon Christ may have fresh supplies from Him for all eternity. They may have an increase of blessedness that is new, and new still, and never will come to an end.

—*Safety, Fullness, and Sweet Refreshment to Be Found in Christ*

QUESTIONS TO CONSIDER

1. Do you ever feel "unacceptable" to God?
2. How can the sweetness of Christ break through that barrier?

A PRAYERFUL RESPONSE

Lord, thank You for Your sweetness that never ends. Amen.

DAY 12

Growing in the Knowledge of God

THOUGHT FOR TODAY
Knowledge apart from God is useless.

WISDOM FROM SCRIPTURE

For this reason, since the day we heard about you, we have not stopped praying for you and asking God to fill you with the knowledge of His will through all spiritual wisdom and understanding.

And we pray this in order that you may live a life worthy of the Lord and may please Him in every way: bearing fruit in every good work, growing in the knowledge of God, being strengthened with all power according to His glorious might so that you may have great endurance and patience, and joyfully giving thanks to the Father, who has qualified you to share in the inheritance of the saints in the kingdom of light.

For He has rescued us from the dominion of darkness and brought us into the kingdom of the Son He loves, in whom we have redemption, the forgiveness of sins.

COLOSSIANS 1:9-14, NIV

INSIGHTS FROM JONATHAN EDWARDS

Every Christian should make a business of growing in the knowledge of God. This is the business of divines and ministers; gaining knowledge by the study of the Scriptures and other instructive books is commonly thought to be their work. Most people seem to think that the knowledge of God may be left to them, and it belongs not to others.

But if the apostle had entertained this notion, he would never have blamed the Christian Hebrews for not having acquired knowledge enough to be teachers. Or if he had thought that this concerned Christians only now and again, and that their time should not be taken up with this business, he never would have so blamed them.

There are two kinds of knowledge of divine truth: speculative and practical. Or in other terms, natural and spiritual.

The former remains only in the head. No other faculty but the understanding is concerned with it. It is obtained by the natural exercise of our own faculties, without any special illumination of the Spirit of God, and consists of a natural or rational knowledge of religion.

The latter rests not entirely in the head or in the speculative ideas of things, but in the heart. Mere intellect, without the will or the inclination, is not the seat of such knowledge, and apprehending it may involve not only seeing but feeling or tasting.

So there is a difference between having a right, speculative notion of the doctrines contained in the Word of God and having a due sense of them in the heart. The former consists of speculative or natural knowledge; the latter consists of spiritual or practical knowledge.

Neither kind of knowledge is intended to exclude the other; it is intended instead that we seek the former to obtain the latter. The latter, the spiritual and practical, is of the greatest importance. A speculative knowledge without a spiritual knowledge has no purpose except to make our condemnation the greater. Yet a speculative knowledge is also of infinite importance, for without it we can have no spiritual or practical knowledge.

The apostle encouraged the Christian Hebrews to seek the first form of knowledge to obtain the second. It is intended that

Christians should, by reading and other proper means, seek a good, rational knowledge of the things of God to obtain the practical knowledge.

God has given us the Bible, which is a book of instructions. But without spiritual understanding, this book can be of no profit to us except as it conveys some knowledge to the mind. It can profit us no more than if it were written in Chinese, of which we know not one word. So the sacraments of the gospel can have a proper effect no other way than by conveying some knowledge. They represent certain things by visible signs. And what is the purpose of signs but to convey some knowledge of the things signified?

Such is the nature of humanity, that nothing can enter the heart except through the door of the understanding. There can be no spiritual knowledge when there is not first a rational knowledge. It is impossible that anyone should see the truth or excellency of any doctrine of the gospel without knowing what that doctrine is. A person cannot see the wonderful excellency and love of Christ in doing such and such things for sinners unless his understanding be first informed how those things were done. He cannot have a taste of the sweetness and excellency of divine truth unless he first have a notion that there is such a thing.

So rational knowledge of God's truth is absolutely necessary. Other kinds of knowledge may be very useful; sciences such as astronomy, natural philosophy, and geography may be very excellent in their kind. But the knowledge of "divine science" is infinitely more useful and important than that of all other sciences whatever.

—*Christian Knowledge*

QUESTIONS TO CONSIDER

1. In what additional ways could you grow in the knowledge of Christ?

2. How can you tell the difference between knowledge and divine wisdom?

A PRAYERFUL RESPONSE

Lord, I open my ears to learn from You. Amen.

The Call to Prayer

THOUGHT FOR TODAY

If we love God, we will spend time with Him in prayer.

WISDOM FROM SCRIPTURE

Rejoice in the Lord always. I will say it again: Rejoice!

Let your gentleness be evident to all. The Lord is near.

Do not be anxious about anything, but in everything, by prayer and petition, with thanksgiving, present your requests to God.

And the peace of God, which transcends all understanding, will guard your hearts and your minds in Christ Jesus.

Finally, brothers, whatever is true, whatever is noble, whatever is right, whatever is pure, whatever is lovely, whatever is admirable—if anything is excellent or praiseworthy—think about such things.

Whatever you have learned or received or heard from me, or seen in me—put it into practice. And the God of peace will be with you.

PHILIPPIANS 4:4-9, NIV

INSIGHTS FROM JONATHAN EDWARDS

I exhort those who have entertained a hope of being true converts, but who since their supposed conversion have left off the duty of secret prayer, to throw away their hope. If you have left off calling upon God, it is time for you to leave off hoping and flattering yourselves that you are the children of God.

The things in people which, if they were known to others,

would be sufficient to convince the world that they are hypocrites, will not convince these people themselves. Likewise, those things which would be sufficient to convince them concerning others, and to cause them to cast others entirely out of their charity, will not be sufficient to convince them concerning themselves. They can make larger allowances for themselves than they can for others. They can find ways to solve objections against their own hope when they can find none in the case of their neighbors.

If your case be such, it is surely time for you to seek a better hope and another work of God's Spirit than you have yet experienced—something more thorough and effectual. When you see that the seed which was sown in your hearts, though at first it sprang up and seemed to flourish, is now withering away from the heat of the sun or is choked with thorns, you will know in what sort of ground the seed was sown. It is either stony or thorny ground, and you will need to pass through another change whereby your heart may become good ground, able to bring forth fruit with patience.

How are your habits consistent with loving God above all? If you have not the spirit to love God above your dearest earthly friends and your most pleasant earthly enjoyments, the Scriptures are very plain that you are not true Christians. But if you had indeed such a spirit, would you grow weary of the practice of drawing near to God and become habitually so averse to it that you would cast off a duty that is so plainly the life of a child of God?

It is the nature of love to be averse to the absence of, and to want a near access to, those we love. We love to be with them; we delight to come often to them and to have much conversation with them. But when a person has been remiss in conversing freely with another—by degrees forsakes him, grows strange, and converses with him but little—it plainly shows a coldness of heart toward him.

The neglect of the duty of prayer seems to be inconsistent with supreme love to God because it is against the plainly revealed will of God. True love to God seeks to please God in everything, and universally to conform to His will.

Consider how inconsistent the neglect of prayer is with leading a holy life. We are abundantly instructed in Scripture that true Christians lead a holy life, and that without holiness no man shall see the Lord (Hebrews 12:14), and that everyone who has this hope in Him purifies himself, even as Christ is pure (1 John 3:3). It is said that the highway of the upright is to depart from evil, the common, beaten road in which all the ungodly travel; and that "a highway shall be there" for the redeemed (Isaiah 35:8). And Romans 8:1 speaks of the character of all believers, that they walk not after the flesh but after the spirit.

How is a life in great measure prayerless consistent with a holy life? To lead a holy life is to lead a life devoted to God, a life of worshipping and serving God, a life consecrated to the service of God. But how can the person who does not even maintain the duty of prayer lead such a life? How can such a person be said to walk by the Spirit and be a servant of the Most High God? A holy life is a life of faith.

The life that true Christians live in the world they live by the faith of the Son of God. But who can believe that the person who lives without prayer truly lives by faith—when the natural expression of faith is prayer? Prayer is as natural an expression of faith as breathing is of life. To say a person lives a life of faith and yet lives a prayerless life is every whit as inconsistent and incredible as to say a person lives without breathing. A prayerless life is so far from being a holy life that it is a profane life. He who lives so lives like a heathen who does not even call on God's name. He who lives a prayerless life lives without God in the world.

—Hypocrites Deficient in the Duty of Prayer

QUESTIONS TO CONSIDER

1. How do you feel about the consistency and quality of your prayer life?
2. Do you want to spend more time in prayer? If so, how can you accomplish this?

A PRAYERFUL RESPONSE

Lord, increase my desire to spend time with You in prayer. Amen.

DAY 14

Many Mansions

THOUGHT FOR TODAY
God promises his children a glorious, eternal home.

WISDOM FROM SCRIPTURE
[Jesus said,] "In my Father's house are many rooms; if it were not so, I would have told you. I am going there to prepare a place for you.

"And if I go and prepare a place for you, I will come back and take you to be with me that you also may be where I am."

JOHN 14:2-3, NIV

Then I saw a new heaven and a new earth, for the first heaven and the first earth had passed away, and there was no longer any sea.

I saw the Holy City, the new Jerusalem, coming down out of heaven from God, prepared as a bride beautifully dressed for her husband.

And I heard a loud voice from the throne saying, "Now the dwelling of God is with men, and He will live with them. They will be His people, and God Himself will be with them and be their God.

"He will wipe every tear from their eyes. There will be no more death or mourning or crying or pain, for the old order of things has passed away."

He who was seated on the throne said, "I am making everything new!" Then He said, "Write this down, for these words are trustworthy and true."

He said to me: "It is done. I am the Alpha and the Omega, the Beginning and the End. To him who is thirsty I will give to drink without cost from the spring of the water of life.

"He who overcomes will inherit all this, and I will be his God and he will be My son.

"But the cowardly, the unbelieving, the vile, the murderers, the sexually immoral, those who practice magic arts, the idolaters and all liars—their place will be in the fiery lake of burning sulfur. This is the second death."

One of the seven angels who had the seven bowls full of the seven last plagues came and said to me, "Come, I will show you the bride, the wife of the Lamb."

And he carried me away in the Spirit to a mountain great and high, and showed me the Holy City, Jerusalem, coming down out of heaven from God.

It shone with the glory of God, and its brilliance was like that of a very precious jewel, like a jasper, clear as crystal.

REVELATION 21:1-11, NIV

INSIGHTS FROM JONATHAN EDWARDS

Heaven is God's house. God is represented in Scripture as a householder or head of a family, and heaven is the house where He dwells with His family. The saints, being the children of God, are of the household of God, and heaven is the place that God has built for them and for Himself. And though some of His children are now on earth, it is only because they are abroad and not yet come home.

Heaven is the house where God has not only His throne but His table—where His children sit down with Him and feast in a royal manner befitting the children of so great a King. God is the King of kings, and heaven is the place where He keeps His court. His angels and archangels attend Him as nobles of his court.

Kings' houses are built very large, with many stately rooms and apartments; and as heaven is a king's palace, there are many mansions in it—many seats or places of abode. There is room in this house for great numbers, for a vast multitude—room enough for all humankind, all who are now or ever shall be. There is room enough in our heavenly Father's house.

And there is mercy enough in God to admit an innumerable multitude into heaven. There is mercy enough for all; and there is merit enough in Christ to purchase heavenly happiness for millions of millions, for all who ever were, are, or shall be. And there is a sufficiency in the fountain of heaven's happiness to supply and fill and satisfy all. There is in all respects enough for the happiness of all.

There are sufficient and suitable accommodations for all the different sorts of persons who are in the world: for great and small, high and low, rich and poor, wise and unwise, bond and free, persons of all nations and all conditions and circumstances; for those who have been great sinners as well as for those who have lived morally; for weak saints and those who are babes in Christ as well as for those who are stronger and more grown in grace. There is in heaven a sufficiency for the happiness of every sort of person.

There is a convenient accommodation for every creature who will hearken to the calls of the gospel. None who come to Christ need fear; Christ will provide a place suitable for him in heaven.

'Tis little worthwhile for us to pursue honor in this world, where the greatest honor is but a bubble and will soon vanish away, and death will level all. Some have more stately houses than others, and some are in higher offices than others, and some are richer than others and have higher seats in the meetinghouse than others; but in the grave they are equal.

But the mansions in God's house are everlasting mansions. Those that have seats allotted there, whether of greater or lesser dignity, whether nearer or farther from the throne, will hold them for all eternity.

If it be worthwhile to desire and seek high seats in the meetinghouse, where you go one day a week and where you shall never come but a few days in all; if it be worthwhile to prize one seat above another in the house of worship only because it is the pew or seat that is ranked first in number, and to be seen there for a few days; how much more worthwhile will it be to seek a high mansion in God's temple and in that glorious place that is the everlasting habitation of God and all His children!

You who are pleased with your seats in this earthly house because you are seated high or in a place that is looked upon honorably by those who sit round about, and because many can behold you, consider how short a time you will enjoy this pleasure. And if there be any who are not happy with their seats because they are too low for them, let them consider that it is only a very little while before it will not matter.

But it will be of infinite and everlasting concern to you where your seat is in another world. Let your great concern while you are in this world be to improve your opportunities in God's house to serve Him, whether you sit high or low. Seek to have a distinguished and glorious mansion in God's house in heaven, where you may be fixed in your place in that glorious assembly in an everlasting rest.

Let the main thing that we prize in God's house be not the outward ornaments of it or a high seat in it but the words and ordinances of God that we hear in it. And spend your time here seeking Christ, that He may prepare a place for you in His Father's house, and that when He comes again to this world He may take you to Himself, that where He is, there you may be also.

—*Many Mansions*

QUESTIONS TO CONSIDER

1. What do you look forward to about living in heaven?
2. How will God's house be better than where you live now?

A PRAYERFUL RESPONSE

Lord, thank You for Your promise of a brand new home. Amen.

PART TWO

The Way to Love

Love Divine, all love excelling,
Joy of heaven, to earth come down;
Fix in us Thy humble dwelling,
All Thy Faithful mercies crown:
Jesus, Thou art all compassion,
Pure, unbounded love Thou art;
Visit us with Thy salvation,
Enter ev'ry trembling heart.

"Love Divine, All Love Excelling"
by Charles Wesley and John Zundel

JONATHAN EDWARDS' INSIGHT
God's unlimited love can fill our hearts and lives.

The Sum of All Virtues

THOUGHT FOR TODAY
Love is the foundation of a living faith.

WISDOM FROM SCRIPTURE

Dear friends, let us love one another, for love comes from God. Everyone who loves has been born of God and knows God.

Whoever does not love does not know God, because God is love.

This is how God showed His love among us: He sent his one and only Son into the world that we might live through Him.

This is love: not that we loved God, but that he loved us and sent his Son as an atoning sacrifice for our sins.

Dear friends, since God so loved us, we also ought to love one another.

No one has ever seen God; but if we love one another, God lives in us and His love is made complete in us.

We know that we live in Him and He in us, because He has given us of His Spirit.

And we have seen and testify that the Father has sent His Son to be the Savior of the world.

If anyone acknowledges that Jesus is the Son of God, God lives in him and he in God.

And so we know and rely on the love God has for us. God is love. Whoever lives in love lives in God, and God in him.

In this way, love is made complete among us so that we will have confidence on the day of judgment, because in this world we are like Him.

There is no fear in love. But perfect love drives out fear, because fear has to do with punishment. The one who fears is not made perfect in love.

We love because He first loved us.

If anyone says, "I love God," yet hates his brother, he is a liar. For anyone who does not love his brother, whom he has seen, cannot love God, whom he has not seen.

And He has given us this command: Whoever loves God must also love his brother.

1 JOHN 4:7-21, NIV

INSIGHTS FROM JONATHAN EDWARDS

Love will dispose people to acts of mercy toward their neighbors when their neighbors face affliction or calamity. We are naturally disposed to pity those we love when they are afflicted. Love will dispose people to give to the poor, to bear one another's burdens, and to weep with those who weep as well as rejoice with those who rejoice.

Love will dispose people to the duties they owe to one another. It will dispose a people to the duties they owe to their rulers, to give them honor and subjection. And it will dispose rulers to rule the people over whom they are set—justly, seriously, and faithfully, seeking their good and not any pursuits of their own. It will dispose a people to all proper duty to their ministers, to hearken to their counsels and instructions, to submit to them in the house of God, and to support, sympathize with, and pray for them as those that watch for their souls.

Love will dispose ministers faithfully and ceaselessly to seek the good of their people's souls, watching out for them as those who must give account. Love will dispose children to honor their parents and servants to be obedient to their masters, not with eye service but in singleness of heart. It will dispose masters to exercise gentleness and goodness toward their servants.

Thus love will affect all duties, both toward God and others. And if it so does, then it follows that love is the root and spring and comprehension of all virtues. It is a principle which, if implanted in the heart, is in itself sufficient to produce all good practice. Every right disposition toward God and others is summed up in love and comes from it, as the fruit from the tree or the stream from the fountain.

If there be no love in what people do, then there is no true respect to God or to others in their conduct; there is no sincerity. Religion is nothing without proper respect to God. The very notion of religion is the creature's exercise and expression of respect toward the Creator. But if there be no true respect or love, then all that is called religion is but a show and there is no real religion in it; it is unreal and vain.

Thus, if a person's faith has no true respect for God, reason teaches that his faith must be in vain. If there be no love for God in it, there can be no true respect for Him. Love is always contained in a true and living faith. Without love, faith is as dead as the body is without its soul. It is love that especially distinguishes a living faith from every other.

Without love to God, again, there can be no true honor to Him. A person is never hearty in the honor he renders to another whom he does not love. Without love, all the seeming honor or worship that is ever paid is hypocritical. And so reason teaches us that there is no sincerity in obedience that is performed without love. If there be no love, nothing that is done can be spontaneous and free; all must be forced.

Without love, there can be no hearty submission to the will

of God, and there can be no real and cordial trust and confidence in Him. He who does not love God will not trust Him. He never will, with true acquiescence of soul, cast himself into the hands of God or into the arms of His mercy.

Whatever good manners there may be in people toward their neighbors, it is unacceptable and in vain if at the same time there be no real respect in the heart toward them—that is, if the outward conduct is not prompted by inward love. All true and distinguishing Christian virtue and grace may be summed up in love.

—All True Grace in the Heart Summed Up
in Charity, or Love

QUESTIONS TO CONSIDER

1. How can you express your love to God?
2. Who in your life needs love today? How can you express your love to them?

A PRAYERFUL RESPONSE

Lord, show me how I can love others as I love You. Amen.

DAY 16

The Most Excellent Gift

THOUGHT FOR TODAY
The greatest gift we can give is love.

WISDOM FROM SCRIPTURE

If I speak in the tongues of mortals and of angels, but do not have love, I am a noisy gong or a clanging cymbal.

And if I have prophetic powers, and understand all mysteries and all knowledge, and if I have all faith, so as to remove mountains, but do not have love, I am nothing. If I give away all my possessions, and if I hand over my body so that I may boast, but do not have love, I gain nothing.

Love is patient; love is kind; love is not envious or boastful or arrogant or rude. It does not rejoice in wrongdoing, but rejoices in the truth.

It bears all things, believes all things, hopes all things, endures all things.

Love never ends. But as for prophecies, they will come to an end; as for tongues, they will cease; as for knowledge, it will come to an end.

For we know only in part; but when the complete comes, the partial will come to an end.

And now faith, hope, and love abide, these three; and the greatest of these is love.

1 CORINTHIANS 13: 1-10, 13, NRSV

The New Testament records an age of miracles. It was not then as it had been of old among the Jews, when only two or three or at most a very few in the whole nation had the gift of prophecy. It rather seemed as if Moses' wish, recorded in Numbers 11:29, had become in great measure fulfilled: "Would to God that all the Lord's people were prophets!"

Not only were certain persons of great eminence endowed with such gifts, but they were common to all sorts, old and young, men and women. It was according to the prophecy of the prophet Joel, who preaching about those days to come foretold the great event: "And it shall come to pass in the last days (saith God), I will pour out of My Spirit upon all flesh: and your sons and your daughters shall prophesy, and your young men shall see visions, and your old men shall dream dreams: and on my servants, and on my handmaidens, I will pour out in those days of My Spirit; and they shall prophesy" (Joel 2:28-29).

The church at Corinth was especially eminent for spiritual gifts. All sorts of miraculous gifts were, as is apparent from this epistle, bestowed on that church. The number who enjoyed these gifts was not small. "To one," says the apostle, "is given by the Spirit the word of wisdom; to another the word of knowledge by the same Spirit; to another faith by the same Spirit; to another the gifts of healing by the same Spirit; to another the working of miracles; to another prophecy; but all these worketh that one and the self-same Spirit, dividing to every man severally as he will" (1 Corinthians 12:8-11). And so some had one gift, and some another.

"But," says the apostle, "covet earnestly the best gifts; and yet show I unto you a more excellent way" (v. 31), something more excellent than all these gifts put together. Yes, something of such great importance that without it all these gifts are nothing. For "though I speak with the tongues of men," as they did on the day of Pentecost, "and of angels," too, "and have not charity, I am become" an empty, worthless thing. I have become "as sounding brass, or a tinkling cymbal." And though I have not just one but all the extraordinary gifts of the Spirit, and not only can speak with tongues but have "the gift of prophecy, and understand all mysteries, and all knowledge" to see into all the deep things of God by immediate inspiration, and though I have all faith to work all sorts of miracles "even so that I could remove mountains, and have not charity, I am nothing" (13:1-2).

Charity, then—the fruit of the ordinary, sanctifying influence of the Holy Spirit—is preferred as being more excellent than any of the extraordinary gifts of the Spirit. Christian love is the sum of all saving grace. Yes, so very much is it preferred that without it all the extraordinary gifts of the Spirit are nothing, and can profit nothing. The influence of the spirit of God, working the grace of charity in our hearts, is a more excellent blessing than any of the extraordinary gifts of the Spirit.

The spiritual image of God is revealed in grace, or holiness—not in the extraordinary gifts of the Spirit, though they are indeed great and mighty endowments from God. The spiritual image of God is not revealed in a power to work miracles and foretell future events, but in being holy, as God is holy—in having holy and divine principles in the heart, influencing us to holy and heavenly lives.

—*Charity or Love, More Excellent Than*
Extraordinary Gifts of the Spirit

QUESTIONS TO CONSIDER

1. What spiritual gifts has God given to you?
2. How can love be integrated into your use of these gifts?

A PRAYERFUL RESPONSE

Lord, thank You for Your unconditional and perfect love. Amen.

All to Be Done With Love

THOUGHT FOR TODAY
God views our hearts through our actions.

WISDOM FROM SCRIPTURE

[Jesus said,] "No good tree bears bad fruit, nor again does a bad tree bear good fruit; for each tree is known by its own fruit. Figs are not gathered from thorns, nor are grapes picked from a bramble bush.

"The good person out of the good treasure of the heart produces good, and the evil person out of the evil treasure produces evil; for it is out of the abundance of the heart that the mouth speaks.

"Why do you call me 'Lord, Lord,' and do not do what I tell you?

"I will show you what someone is like who comes to Me, hears My words, and acts on them.

"That one is like a man building a house, who dug deeply and laid the foundation on rock; when a flood arose, the river burst against that house but could not shake it, because it had been well built.

"But the one who hears and does not act is like a man who built a house on the ground without a foundation. When the river burst against it, immediately it fell, and great was the ruin of that house."

LUKE 6:43-49, NRSV

Whatever people may do or suffer, they cannot by all their performances and sufferings make up for the want of sincere love in the heart. If they are engaged in acts of justice and kindness and devotion, if their prayers and fastings are multiplied, if they should spend their time in the forms of religious worship, giving days and nights to it—it would all be in vain without sincere love for God in the heart.

So if a person should give most bounteously to religious or charitable uses, and if, possessing the riches of a kingdom, he should give it all, and from the splendor of an earthly prince should reduce himself to a level of beggars, even all this would not make up for the want of sincere love for God in the heart.

It is not the external work done or the suffering endured that is, in itself, worth anything in the sight of God. The motions and exercise of the body, or anything that may be done by the body, if considered separately from the heart is of no more consequence or worth in the sight of God than the motions of anything without life.

If anything be offered or given—silver or gold or the cattle on a thousand hills, a thousand rams or ten thousand rivers of oil—in God's sight there is nothing of value in it as an external thing. If God were in need of these things, they might be of value to Him in themselves, independent of the motives of the heart. We humans often stand in need of external good things; therefore such things offered or given to us may and do have a value to us in themselves.

But God stands in need of nothing. He is all-sufficient in Himself. And as there is nothing profitable to God in any of our services or performances, so there can be nothing acceptable in His sight without sincere love in the heart. "For the Lord seeth not as men seeth; for man looketh on the outward appearance, but God looketh on the heart" (1 Samuel 16:7). The heart is just as naked and open to Him as are external actions. And therefore He sees our actions, and all our conduct, not merely as the external motions of a machine but as the actions of rational, intelligent creatures and voluntary free agents. Therefore, if the heart be not right, there can be in God's estimation no excellence or amiableness in anything we can do.

He who has no sincerity in his heart has no real respect for God in what he seems to give, nor in all his performances or sufferings. If his aim be his own honor, ease, or worldly profit, then the gift is but an offering to these things, not to God. The gift is an offering to him to whom the giver's heart devotes himself, and for whom he designs it. It is the aim of the heart that makes the reality of the gift. And if the sincere aim of the heart is not to please God, then there is in reality nothing given to Him, no matter what is performed or suffered.

It would be a great absurdity to suppose that anything offered or given to God can make up for the absence of love in the heart toward Him. For without this, nothing is truly given, and the seeming gift is but a mockery of the Most High. This love or charity is the sum of all that God requires of us. And it is absurd to suppose that anything can make up for the want of that which is the sum of all that God requires.

Charity or love is something that has its seat in the heart, and consists of all that is saving and distinguishing in Christian character. If we make a great show of respect and love to God in our outward actions while there is no sincerity in our hearts, it is but hypocrisy and practical lying unto the Holy One.

—All That Can Be Done or Suffered Is in Vain
Without Charity, or Love

QUESTIONS TO CONSIDER

1. How can you know if your actions are motivated by love?
2. How can sincere love enhance your spiritual acts and attitudes?

A PRAYERFUL RESPONSE

Lord, let all I do in Your name be motivated by love. Amen.

Blessed Are the Meek

THOUGHT FOR TODAY
A meek heart loves deeply.

WISDOM FROM SCRIPTURE

[Jesus said,] "You have heard that it was said, 'An eye for an eye and a tooth for a tooth.'

"But I say to you, Do not resist an evildoer. But if anyone strikes you on the right cheek, turn the other also; and if anyone wants to sue you and take your coat, give your cloak as well; and if anyone forces you to go one mile, go also the second mile.

"Give to everyone who begs from you, and do not refuse anyone who wants to borrow from you.

"You have heard that it was said, 'You shall love your neighbor and hate your enemy.'

"But I say to you, Love your enemies and pray for those who persecute you, so that you may be children of your Father in heaven; for He makes the sun rise on the evil and on the good, and sends rain on the righteous and on the unrighteous.

"For if you love those who love you, what reward do you have? Do not even the tax collectors do the same?

"And if you greet only your brothers and sisters, what more are you doing than others? Do not even the Gentiles do the same?

"Be perfect, therefore, as your heavenly Father is perfect."

MATTHEW 5:38-48, NRSV

Meekness is a great part of the Christian spirit. Christ invites all that labor and are heavy laden to come to Him for rest, and He adds, "I am meek and lowly in heart" (Matthew 11:29). Meekness, as it respects injuries received from others, is called long-suffering in the Scriptures and is often mentioned as a fruit of the Spirit.

Love for God disposes us to imitate Him, and therefore disposes us to the long-suffering He manifests. Long-suffering is also one of the attributes of God. In Exodus 34:6 we read, "And the Lord passed by before him, and proclaimed, the Lord, the Lord God, merciful and gracious, long-suffering." And in Romans 2:4 the apostle asks, "Despisest thou the riches of His goodness and forbearance and long-suffering?"

The long-suffering of God is wonderfully manifested in His bearing of innumerable injuries from His enemies, injuries that are great and longcontinued. If we consider the wickedness in the world, and then consider how God continues the world in existence and does not destroy it, but showers upon it innumerable mercies—the bounties of His daily providence and grace, such as causing His sun to rise on the evil and on the good, and sending rain alike on the just and on the unjust, and offering His spiritual blessings ceaselessly and to all—then we shall perceive how abundant is His long-suffering toward us.

And if we consider God's long-suffering to some of the great and populous cities of the world, and think how constantly the gifts of His goodness are bestowed on and consumed by them, and then consider how great the wickedness of these cities is, it will show us how amazingly great is His long-suffering.

The same long-suffering has been manifested to many persons in all ages of the world. He is long-suffering to the sinners that He spares, and to whom He offers His mercy—even while they are rebelling against Him. He was long-suffering toward His own elect people, many of whom lived in sin and despised His goodness and His wrath. Yet He bore long with them, even to the end, till they were brought to repentance and made, through His grace, vessels of mercy and glory. And this mercy He showed to them even while they were enemies and rebels, as the apostle Paul tells us was the case with himself.

Love for God promotes humility, which is one main root of a meek and long-suffering spirit. Love for God, as it exalts Him, promotes low thoughts and estimates of ourselves, and leads to a deep sense of our unworthiness. He who loves God is sensible of the hatefulness and vileness of sin committed against the Being whom he loves. And discerning an abundance of this in himself, he abhors himself in his own eyes as unworthy of any good, and deserving of all evil.

Humility is always found connected with long-suffering, as the apostle says in Ephesians 4:2: "With all lowliness and meekness, with long-suffering, forbearing one another in love." A humble spirit disinclines us to indulge in resentment, for he who is little and unworthy in his own eyes will not think so much of an injury someone else inflicts on him. It is deemed a greater and higher enormity to offend one who is great and high than one who is lowly and vile.

Some may be ready to say that the injuries they receive from others are intolerable; that the one who has injured them has been so unreasonable in what he has said or done, and it is so unjust and injurious and unjustifiable that it is more than flesh and blood can bear. They feel treated with so much injustice that it is enough to provoke a stone; with such contempt that they are actually trampled on; and they cannot but resent it. But in answer to this objection, I would ask a few questions.

First, do you think the injuries you have received from others are more than you have inflicted on God? Has your enemy been more base, more unreasonable, more ungrateful, than you have been to the High and Holy One? Second, do you not hope that God will continue to bear with you in your shortcomings as He has in the past, and that in spite of everything, He will exercise toward you His infinite love and favor? Third, when you think of such long-suffering on God's part, do you not approve of and think well of it, not only as worthy and excellent but as exceeding glorious? Fourth, if such a course be excellent and worthy enough to be approved of in God, why is it not so in yourself? Why should you not imitate it?

Therefore we are compelled to love others with the meekness and humility that God extends to us, who are unworthy of such love.

—*Charity Meek in Bearing Evil and Injuries*

QUESTIONS TO CONSIDER
1. Why do we often define meek the same as "weak"?
2. Why would God ask us to give so much in loving others?

A PRAYERFUL RESPONSE
Lord, help me to love others with the meekness and humility with which You love me. Amen.

DAY 19

Cheerfulness in Doing Good

THOUGHT FOR TODAY
The Lord asks us to do good to all.

WISDOM FROM SCRIPTURE

My friends, if anyone is detected in a transgression, you who have received the Spirit should restore such a one in a spirit of gentleness. Take care that you yourselves are not tempted.

Bear one another's burdens and in this way you will fulfill the law of Christ.

For if those who are nothing think they are something, they deceive themselves.

All must test their own work; then that work, rather than their neighbor's work, will become a cause for pride.

For all must carry their own loads.

Those who are taught the word must share in all good things with their teacher.

Do not be deceived; God is not mocked, for you reap whatever you sow.

If you sow to your own flesh, you will reap corruption from the flesh; but if you sow to the Spirit, you will reap eternal life from the Spirit.

So let us not grow weary in doing what is right, for we will reap at harvest time, if we do not give up.

So then, whenever we have an opportunity, let us work for the good of all, and especially for those of the family of faith.

GALATIANS 6:1-10, NRSV

We are to do good both to the good and the bad among us. This we are to do as we imitate our heavenly Father, for "He maketh His sun to rise on the evil and on the good, and sendeth rain on the just and on the unjust" (Matthew 5:43-45). The world is full of various kinds of persons, some good and some evil, and we should do good to all. We should especially "do good to them that are of the household of faith" (Galatians 6:10), whom we are to regard as saints. But though we should most abound in charity to them, yet our doing good should not be confined to them. We should do good to all as we have opportunity.

In the world we must expect to meet with some evil people of hateful dispositions and practices. Some are proud, some immoral, some covetous, some profane, some unjust or severe, and some despisers of God. But any or all of these bad qualities should not hinder our charity nor prevent our doing them good as we have opportunity. On this account we should be diligent to benefit them: that we may win them to Christ; and especially should we be diligent to benefit them in spiritual things.

Second, we should do good both to friends and enemies. We are obliged to do good to our friends not only out of obligation because they are our fellow creatures, made in the image of God, but also out of friendship, gratitude, and affection.

We are also to do good to our enemies, for our Savior says in Matthew 5:44, "But I say unto you, Love your enemies; bless them that curse you; do good to them that hate you; and pray for them that despitefully use you, and persecute you." To do good to those who do ill to us is the only retaliation that becomes us as Christians. We are taught to "recompense to no man evil for evil," but on the contrary to "overcome evil with good" (Romans 12:17-21). Again, it is written, "See that none render evil for evil unto any man; but ever follow that which is good, both among yourselves, and to all men" (1 Thessalonians 5:15). And still again, "Not rendering evil for evil, or railing for railing: but contrariwise blessing; knowing that ye are thereunto called, that ye should inherit a blessing" (1 Peter 3:9).

The manner in which we should do good to others is expressed in the single word "freely." This seems implied in the words of the text; for to be kind is to do good freely. Whatever good is done, there is no proper kindness in it unless it is done freely. And this doing good freely implies three things.

First, our doing good must not be in a mercenary spirit. We are not to do good for the sake of any reward received or expected from the one to whom we do the good. Oftentimes people will do good to others expecting to receive as much again, but we should do good to the poor and needy, from whom we can expect nothing in return. To make certain that our doing good is truly free, and not mercenary, whatever we do, we must do it not for the sake of any temporal good or to promote our temporal interest, honor, or profit, but from the spirit of love.

Second, to make certain that our doing good is free, we must do it cheerfully or heartily, and with real goodwill. What is done heartily is done from love. What is done from love is done with delight, not grudgingly or with backwardness and reluctance of spirit. This requisite or qualification for our doing good is much insisted on in the Scriptures. The very idea of acceptable giving is presented throughout the Bible as giving with a cordial and cheerful spirit.

Doing good freely also implies, third, that we do it liberally and bountifully. We are not to be scant and sparing in our gifts or efforts, but open-hearted and open-handed. We are to "abound to every good work" and be "enriched in everything to all bountifulness" (2 Corinthians 9:8-11). Thus God requires that when we give to the poor, we should "open our hand wide unto him" (Deuteronomy 15:8), and we are told that "the liberal soul shall be made fat" (Proverbs 11:25). The apostle encouraged the Corinthians to be bountiful in their contributions to the poor saints in Judea, assuring them that "he which soweth sparingly shall reap also sparingly, and he which soweth bountifully shall reap also bountifully" (2 Corinthians 9:6).

The main thing in Christian love is benevolence, or goodwill to others. Benevolence is that disposition which leads us to have a desire for or to take delight in the good of another. That is the main thing in Christian love—yes, the most essential thing in it. Our love is to be an imitation of the eternal love and grace of God and of the dying love of Christ, which consists of benevolence or goodwill to men, as was sung by the angels at his birth (Luke 2:14). Christian love is goodwill—a spirit to delight in and seek the good of those who are the objects of that love.

—Charity Cheerful and Free in Doing Good

QUESTIONS TO CONSIDER

1. How can you sow goodness among those around you?
2. Specifically, how can you imitate Christ's love to someone today?

A PRAYERFUL RESPONSE

Lord, I will sow goodness wherever You lead me. Amen.

Love Does Not Envy

THOUGHT FOR TODAY
Through love, we can rejoice in the good fortune of others.

WISDOM FROM SCRIPTURE
Owe no one anything, except to love one another; for the one who loves another has fulfilled the law.

The commandments, "You shall not commit adultery; You shall not murder; You shall not steal; You shall not covet"; and any other commandment, are summed up in this word, "Love your neighbor as yourself."

Love does no wrong to a neighbor; therefore, love is the fulfilling of the law.

Besides this, you know what time it is, how it is now the moment for you to wake from sleep. For salvation is nearer to us now than when we became believers; the night is far gone, the day is near. Let us then lay aside the works of darkness and put on the armor of light; let us live honorably as in the day, not in reveling and drunkenness, not in debauchery and licentiousness, not in quarreling and jealousy.

Instead, put on the Lord Jesus Christ, and make no provision for the flesh, to gratify its desires.

ROMANS 13:8-14, NRSV

Christian love disposes us to hearken to the precepts that forbid envy. The nature of charity or Christian love toward others is directly contrary to envy, for love does not grudge but rejoices at the good of those who are loved. And surely love to our neighbor does not dispose us to hate him for his prosperity or be unhappy at his good fortune.

Love for God also compels us to obey His commands. The natural fruit of love for God is obedience, and therefore obedience follows those commands wherein God forbids envy. Love delights to obey no commands so much as those that require love. And so love for God will dispose us to follow His example in this: that He has not begrudged us our many blessings but has rejoiced in our enjoyment. Love for God will dispose us to imitate the example of Christ in not begrudging His life for our sakes and to imitate the example He set for us in His life on earth.

A spirit of Christian love also inclines us toward humility. Pride is the great root and source of envy. It is because of the pride in people's hearts that they have such a burning desire to be distinguished and to be superior to others in honor and prosperity. It makes them uneasy and dissatisfied to see others above them. But a spirit of love tends to bring down pride and work humility into the heart.

Love for God promotes humility, as it implies a sense of God's infinite excellence, and therefore we sense our comparative nothingness and unworthiness. Love for others also promotes humility, as it disposes us to acknowledge the excellencies of others, to recognize that the honors bestowed on them are their due, and to esteem them better than ourselves—and thus more deserving of distinction than we are.

Humility should lead us to examine ourselves to see if we are in any degree under the influence of an envious spirit. Let us examine ourselves as to time past and look over our past behavior. Many of us have long been members of human society, living with others and associating with them in many ways, both in public and private affairs. And we have seen others in prosperity—perhaps prospering in their affairs more than ourselves. They have perhaps had more in the world, and possessed greater riches, and lived in greater ease and much more honorable circumstances than we have enjoyed. We may have seen some people we used to look upon as our equals, or even as inferiors, growing in wealth or advancing in honor and prosperity while we have been left behind, until now they have reached a station far superior to our own. It may be that we have seen such changes and been called to bear such trials through a great part of our life.

And turning from the past to the present, what spirit do you find as you search your heart? Do you carry any old grudge in your heart against someone you see sitting with you from Sabbath to Sabbath in the house of God, and from time to time sitting with you at the Lord's table? Is the prosperity of one or another an eyesore to you? Does it make you uncomfortable that some are higher than you? Would it be a comfort to see them brought down, so their losses and depression would be a source of inward joy to your heart?

But it may be that in all this you justify yourself, not giving it the name of envy but some other name, and having various excuses for your envious spirit, you account yourself justified. Some are ready to say that others are not worthy of the honor and prosperity they have—that they have not half the fitness or worthiness of their honor and advancement as many of their neighbors.

You remember the spirit of Cain toward Abel, of the seed of the serpent toward the seed of the woman, of Ishmael toward Isaac, of the Jews toward Christ, of the elder brother toward the prodigal? Beware that you cherish not their spirit, but rather rejoice in the good estate of others as much as if it were your own.

—*The Spirit of Charity the Opposite of an Envious Spirit*

QUESTIONS TO CONSIDER

1. Do you envy anyone? Why?
2. How can you change that envy to love?

A PRAYERFUL RESPONSE

Lord, help me to take my eyes off others and keep them on You. Amen.

DAY 21

Walking in Humility

THOUGHT FOR TODAY

Humble people understand their place with God and others.

WISDOM FROM SCRIPTURE

If then there is any encouragement in Christ, any consolation from love, any sharing in the Spirit, any compassion and sympathy, make my joy complete: be of the same mind, having the same love, being in full accord and of one mind.

Do nothing from selfish ambition or conceit, but in humility regard others as better than yourselves.

Let each of you look not to your own interests, but to the interests of others.

Let the same mind be in you that was in Christ Jesus, who, though he was in the form of God, did not regard equality with God as something to be exploited, but emptied himself, taking the form of a slave, being born in human likeness. And being found in human form, He humbled Himself and became obedient to the point of death—even death on a cross.

Therefore God also highly exalted Him and gave Him the name that is above every name, so that at the name of Jesus every knee should bend, in heaven and on earth and under the earth, and every tongue should confess that Jesus Christ is Lord, to the glory of God the Father.

PHILIPPIANS 2:1-11, NRSV

Love is not proud. On the one hand, it prevents us from envying what others possess; on the other, it keeps us from glorying in what we ourselves possess. When people have obtained prosperity or advancement and others observe that they are puffed up and vaunt themselves in it, their behavior tends to provoke envy and make others uneasy.

But if a person has prosperity or advancement but does not vaunt himself or behave in an unseemly manner on account of it, his modesty tends to reconcile others to his high circumstances and make them satisfied that he should enjoy his elevation. Christian love tends to make all persons behave suitably to their condition: if below others, not to envy them, and if above others, not to be proud or puffed up with the prosperity.

A spirit of Christian love is the opposite of proud behavior, of which two degrees exist. The higher degree of pride is expressed by a person's "vaunting himself," that is, by showing plainly that he glories in what he has or who he is. The lower degree is expressed by his "behaving himself unseemly," that is, by acting as if his prosperity exalts him above others. The spirit of charity or love is opposed not only to proud behavior but to a proud spirit or pride in the heart, for charity "is not puffed up" (1 Corinthians 13:4). This spirit of charity or Christian love is a humble spirit.

The first step toward humility is gaining a sense of our own comparative lowliness. I say comparative lowliness, because humility is a grace proper for those who are glorious and excellent in many respects. Thus the saints and angels in heaven excel in humility, and humility is proper and suitable in them even though they are pure, spotless, and glorious beings, perfect in holiness and excelling in mind and strength. But though they are glorious, still they have a comparative lowliness before God.

Even the man Christ Jesus, who is the most excellent and glorious of all creatures, is yet meek and lowly of heart and excels all other beings in humility. Humility is one of the excellencies of Christ, because He is not only God but man, and as a man He was humble.

Humility is not and cannot be an attribute of the divine nature. God's nature is indeed infinitely opposite to pride, and yet neither can humility properly be attributed to Him. If it could, it would argue imperfection, which is impossible in God. God, who is infinite in excellence and glory and infinitely above all things, cannot have any comparative lowliness and therefore does not need humility.

Humility is proper to all created intelligent beings, for they are all infinitely little before God, and most of them are in some way low in comparison with some of their fellow creatures. Humility implies that we think not of ourselves more highly than we ought to think, but that we think soberly, according as God has dealt to every one of us the measure not only of faith but of other things (Romans 12:3). And this humility implies a sense of our own comparative lowliness, both as compared with God and as compared with our fellow creatures.

He who has a right sense and estimate of himself in comparison with God will be likely to have his eyes open to see himself aright in all respects. Seeing truly how he stands with respect to the first and highest of all beings will tend greatly to help him understand the place he stands among creatures. And he who does not rightly know the first and greatest of beings, the Fountain and Source of all other beings, cannot truly know anything aright.

—*The Spirit of Charity an Humble Spirit*

QUESTIONS TO CONSIDER

1. How do you estimate yourself in relation to God and to others?
2. How might it be a challenge to stay in right relationship to others—not too "high" or too "low"?

A PRAYERFUL RESPONSE

Lord, show me a place of right relationship to You and others. Amen.

DAY 22

Love Without Selfishness

THOUGHT FOR TODAY
True love considers the needs of others as vital as its own.

WISDOM FROM SCRIPTURE
With it [the tongue] we bless the Lord and Father, and with it we curse those who are made in the likeness of God.

From the same mouth come blessing and cursing. My brothers and sisters, this ought not to be so.

Does a spring pour forth from the same opening both fresh and brackish water?

Can a fig tree, my brothers and sisters, yield olives, or a grapevine fig? No more can salt water yield fresh.

Who is wise and understanding among you? Show by your good life that your works are done with gentleness born of wisdom.

But if you have bitter envy and selfish ambition in your hearts, do not be boastful and false to the truth.

Such wisdom does not come down from above, but is earthly, unspiritual, devilish.

For where there is envy and selfish ambition, there will also be disorder and wickedness of every kind.

But the wisdom from above is first pure, then peaceable, gentle, willing to yield, full of mercy and good fruits, without a trace of partiality or hypocrisy.

And a harvest of righteousness is sown in peace for those who make peace.

JAMES 3:9-18, NRSV

It is not contrary to Christianity that a person should love himself, or that he should love his own happiness, which is the same thing. If Christianity did indeed destroy a person's love for himself and for his own happiness, it would destroy the very spirit of humanity. The announcement of the gospel as a system of peace on earth and goodwill toward men (Luke 2:14) shows that it is not destructive of humanity but in the highest degree promotive of its spirit.

That a person should love his own happiness is as necessary to his nature as the faculty of his will. It is impossible that such a love should be destroyed in any other way than by destroying his being. The saints love their own happiness. Yes, those who are perfect in happiness, the saints and angels in heaven, love their own happiness. Otherwise, the happiness that God has given them would be no happiness to them, for that which anyone does not love he cannot enjoy.

To love ourselves is not unlawful. The law of God makes self-love a rule and measure by which our love to others should be regulated. Thus Christ commands, "Thou shalt love thy neighbour as thyself" (Matthew 19:19), which certainly supposes that we may, and must, love ourselves. It is not said *more* than thyself, but *"as* thyself." But we are commanded to love our neighbor next to God; therefore we are to love ourselves with a love next to that which we should exercise toward God Himself.

The same appears from the fact that the Scriptures, from one end of the Bible to the other, are full of incentives set forth for the purpose of working on the principle of self-love. Such are all the promises and warnings of the Word of God, its calls and invitations, its counsels to seek our own good and its warnings to beware of misery.

Persons may also place their happiness in the good of others and, desiring the happiness that comes from seeking good for others, may, in seeking it, also love themselves and their own happiness. And yet this is not selfishness, because it is not a confined self-love. The individual's self-love flows out in such a channel as to take in others with himself. The self that he loves is, as it were, enlarged and multiplied so that in the very acts in which he loves himself, he loves others also.

This is the Christian spirit, the excellent and noble spirit of the gospel of Jesus Christ. A Christian spirit is contrary to that selfish spirit of self-love that seeks such objects as worldly wealth, or the honor of being set up higher in the world than one's neighbors, or one's own worldly ease and convenience, or the gratification of one's own bodily appetites and lusts.

A spirit of charity or Christian love, as exercised toward our fellow creatures, is the opposite of a selfish spirit. It is a sympathizing and merciful spirit. It disposes persons to consider not only their own difficulties but also the burdens and afflictions of others and the difficulties of their circumstances; it disposes them to esteem the case of those who are in straits and necessities like their own.

A person of selfish spirit is ready to make much of the afflictions he is under, as if his privations or sufferings were greater than those of anybody else. And if he is not suffering, he is ready to think he is not called to spare what he possesses for the sake of helping others. A selfish person is not apt to discern the wants of others but rather to overlook them—indeed, he can hardly be persuaded to see or feel them. But a person of charitable spirit is apt to see the afflictions of others, and to take notice of their aggravation, and to be as filled with concern for them as he would be for himself if under difficulties. And he is ready also to help them and to take delight in supplying their necessities and relieving their difficulties.

Just as the spirit of charity or Christian love, in that it is merciful and liberal, is opposed to a selfish spirit, so it disposes a person to be public-spirited. A person of a right spirit is not one who has narrow and private views; he is greatly interested and concerned for the good of the community to which he belongs, particularly of the city or village in which he resides, and for the true welfare of the society of which he is a member.

Those possessed of the spirit of Christian charity have a more enlarged spirit still. They are concerned not only for the thrift of the community but for the welfare of the Church of God, and of all the people of God individually.

—*The Spirit of Charity the Opposite of a Selfish Spirit*

QUESTIONS TO CONSIDER

1. How do you feel about Edwards' belief that we're to love ourselves?
2. How might loving yourself affect your loving others?

A PRAYERFUL RESPONSE

Lord, I desire to love others with an unselfish love. Amen.

DAY 23

No Room for Anger

THOUGHT FOR TODAY
Without great care, it is easy for anger to lead to sin.

WISDOM FROM SCRIPTURE
So then, putting away falsehood, let all of us speak the truth to our neighbors, for we are members of one another.

Be angry but do not sin; do not let the sun go down on your anger, and do not make room for the devil.

Thieves must give up stealing; rather let them labor and work honestly with their own hands, so as to have something to share with the needy.

Let no evil talk come out of your mouths, but only what is useful for building up as there is need, so that your words may give grace to those who hear.

And do not grieve the Holy Spirit of God, with which you were marked with a seal for the day of redemption.

Put away from you all bitterness and wrath and anger and wrangling and slander, together with all malice, and be kind to one another, tenderhearted, forgiving one another, as God in Christ has forgiven you.

Therefore be imitators of God, as beloved children, and live in love, as Christ loved us and gave Himself up for us, a fragrant offering and sacrifice to God.

EPHESIANS 4:25–5:2, NRSV

Christianity is not opposite and contrary to all anger. Ephesians 4:26 says, "Be ye angry, and sin not," which seems to suggest that there is such a thing as anger without sin, or that it is possible to be angry in some cases and still not offend God. However, a Christian spirit, the spirit of charity, is the opposite of *unsuitable* anger.

Anger may be defined as an earnest and violent opposition of spirit toward any real or supposed evil, or in regard to any fault or offense of another. All anger is opposition of the mind to real or supposed evil, but not all opposition of the mind to evil is properly called anger. There is an opposition of judgment that is not anger; for anger is the opposition not of cool judgment but of the spirit or heart. But here again, not all opposition of the spirit toward evil can be called anger.

The opposition of the spirit to natural evil such as grief and sorrow, for instance, is a very different thing from anger. Anger is opposition to moral evil, real or supposed, in voluntary agents, or at least in agents that are conceived to be voluntary or acting by their own will. But yet again, not all opposition of the spirit to evil is anger. There may be a dislike, without the spirit being excited and angry; and such dislike is in opposition to the will and judgment.

In all anger there must be earnestness and opposition of feeling, and the spirit must be moved and stirred within us. Anger is one of the passions or affections of the soul, though when called an affection it is for the most part to be regarded as an evil affection.

All anger that contains ill will or a desire for revenge is unsuitable anger. Some have defined anger as a desire for revenge, but this cannot be considered a just definition of anger in general. If it were so, all anger would imply ill will and the desire that some other might be injured. But anger may be consistent with goodwill.

A father may find himself in opposition to the bad conduct of his child, for example, and his spirit may be engaged and stirred in opposition to that conduct. At the same time, he will not have any ill will to the child, but on the contrary a real goodwill. Far from desiring his child's injury, he may have the highest desire for its true welfare, and his very anger is opposition to what will be injurious to it. Anger, in its general nature, consists in the opposition of the spirit to evil rather than in a desire for revenge.

We are required by Christ to wish others well and to pray for the prosperity of all, even our enemies and those who despitefully use and persecute us (Matthew 5:44). The rule given by the apostle is, "Bless them which persecute you: bless, and curse not" (Romans 12:14). That is, we are only to wish and pray for good to others—and in no case to wish evil. All revenge is forbidden except for the vengeance which public justice takes on transgressors. In the infliction of public justice, humans act not for themselves but for God.

So Christianity is contrary to all anger that contains ill will or a desire for revenge, and strongly forbids it. Sometimes anger as it is spoken of in Scripture is meant only in the worst sense, in that sense which implies ill will and the desire for revenge. In this sense all anger is forbidden.

We should never be angry except at sin, and sin should always be that which we oppose in our anger. When our spirits are stirred to oppose evil, it should be chiefly the sin against God that we oppose. If there be no sin and no fault, we have no cause to be angry. Persons sin in their anger when they are selfish in it. We are not to act for ourselves simply, as if we were our own, for we belong to God and not to ourselves. When a fault is committed wherein God is sinned against and people are injured, we should be chiefly concerned with it and our spirits chiefly moved against it because it is committed against God. We should be more desirous of God's honor than of our own temporal interests.

All anger is either a virtue or a vice; there is no middle sort. There is no virtue or goodness in opposing sin unless it be opposed *as* sin. Virtuous anger is the same thing which in one form is called zeal. Our anger should be like Christ's anger. He was like a lamb under the greatest personal injuries, and we never read of his being angry except in the cause of God against sin as sin. And this should be the case with us.

—*The Spirit of Charity the Opposite of*
an Angry or Wrathful Spirit

QUESTIONS TO CONSIDER

1. What makes you most angry? Why?
2. How can you keep your anger from causing you to sin?

A PRAYERFUL RESPONSE

Lord, direct my anger at sin only, so that I may not sin. Amen.

No Place for Criticism

THOUGHT FOR TODAY
A critical spirit tears down those around us.

WISDOM FROM SCRIPTURE
Welcome those who are weak in faith, but not for the purpose of quarreling over opinions.

Some believe in eating anything, while the weak eat only vegetables.

Those who eat must not despise those who abstain, and those who abstain must not pass judgment on those who eat; for God has welcomed them.

Who are you to pass judgment on servants of another? It is before their own lord that they stand or fall. And they will be upheld, for the Lord is able to make them stand.

Some judge one day to be better than another while others judge all days to be alike. Let all be fully convinced in their own minds.

Those who observe the day, observe it in honor of the Lord. Also those who eat, eat in honor of the Lord, since they give thanks to God; while those who abstain, abstain in honor of the Lord and give thanks to God.

We do not live to ourselves, and we do not die to ourselves.

If we live, we live to the Lord, and if we die, we die to the Lord; so then, whether we live or whether we die, we are the Lord's.

For to this end Christ died and lived again, so that he might be Lord of both the dead and the living.

Why do you pass judgement on your brother or sister? Or you, why do you despise your brother or sister? For we will all stand before the judgment seat of God.

ROMANS 14:1-10, NRSV

INSIGHTS FROM JONATHAN EDWARDS

A critical spirit manifests a proud spirit. And this is contrary to the spirit of charity or Christian love. An inclination to judge and censure others shows a proud disposition, as though the critical person thinks himself free from such faults and blemishes and therefore feels justified in being bitter and critical. This is implied in the language of the Savior, "Judge not, that ye be not judged. And why beholdest thou the mote that is in thy brother's eye, but considerest not the beam that is in thine own eye? Or how wilt thou say to thy brother, 'Let me pull out the mote out of thine eye'; and, behold, a beam is in thine own eye? Thou hypocrite!" (Matthew 7:1, 3-5).

If people were humbly sensible of their own failings, they would not be so inclined to judge others, for the censure passed upon others would rest on themselves. The same kinds of corruption exist in one person's heart as in another's. If those persons who are busy censuring others would look within and seriously examine their own hearts and lives, they might see the same dispositions and behavior in themselves, at one time or another, which they see and judge in others—or at least something as much deserving of censure.

A propensity to judge and condemn shows a conceited and arrogant disposition. It has the appearance of a person's setting himself up above others as though he were fit to be the lord and judge of his fellow servants, and expecting them to stand or fall according to his sentence. This seems implied in the language of the apostle: "He that speaketh evil of his brother, and judgeth his brother, speaketh evil of the law, and judgeth the law; but if thou judge the law, thou art not a doer of the law, but a judge" (James 4:11). That is, you do not act as a fellow servant to the person you judge or as one who is under the same law that you are, but as the giver of the law and the judge whose province it is to pass sentence under it.

Therefore the next verse adds, "There is one lawgiver, who is able to save and to destroy. Who art thou that judgest another?" And so in Romans 14:4: "Who art thou that judgest another man's servant? To his own master he standeth or falleth." God is the only rightful judge, and the thought of his sovereignty and dominion should hold us back from daring to judge or censure others.

Scripture sternly reproves those who commonly speak evil of others. If to think evil is condemned, surely they are more to be condemned who allow themselves not only to think but also to *speak* evil things of others, backbiting them with their tongues. Evil-speaking against neighbors behind their backs or expressing uncharitable thoughts and judgments of their persons and behavior is the same as censuring them. As in the passage just quoted from the apostle James, in the Bible, speaking evil of others and judging others are sometimes the same thing.

Scripture often condemns backbiting and evil-speaking. Consider, therefore, whether you yourselves have been guilty of this; whether you have frequently criticized others–especially those with whom you may have had difficulty, or who are different from you. Is it not a practice you more or less allow yourself even now, from day to day? If so, consider how contrary it is to the spirit of Christianity, and forsake it immediately.

How often, on thorough examination, have we found others better than what we have heard about them? There are always two sides to every story, and it is generally wise and safe and charitable to believe the best about others. Yet there is probably no one way in which persons are so liable to be wrong as in presuming that the worst is true, and in forming and expressing their judgment of others, without waiting till all the truth is known. Therefore, as we would not ourselves want condemnation from others, let us not condemn nor criticize others.

—The Spirit of Charity the Opposite
of a Critical Spirit

QUESTIONS TO CONSIDER
1. What makes you feel critical toward others? Why?
2. How do you feel when others criticize you?

A PRAYERFUL RESPONSE
Lord, show me when I am critical toward others. Amen.

DAY 25

The Practice of Holiness

THOUGHT FOR TODAY
We were created to be holy before God.

WISDOM FROM SCRIPTURE
Therefore prepare your minds for action; discipline yourselves; set all your hope on the grace that Jesus Christ will bring you when He is revealed.

Like obedient children, do not be conformed to the desires that you formerly had in ignorance.

Instead, as He who called you is holy, be holy yourselves in all your conduct; for it is written, "You shall be holy, for I am holy."

If you invoke as Father the one who judges all people impartially according to their deeds, live in reverent fear during the time of your exile.

You know that you were ransomed from the futile ways inherited from your ancestors, not with perishable things like silver or gold, but with the precious blood of Christ, like that of a lamb without defect or blemish.

He was destined before the foundation of the world, but was revealed at the end of the ages for your sake.

Through Him you have come to trust in God, who raised Him from the dead and gave Him glory, so that your faith and hope are set on God.

Now that you have purified your souls by your obedience to the truth so that you have genuine mutual love, love one another deeply from the heart.

1 PETER 1:13-22, NRSV

God, by His Spirit and through His truth, calls, awakens, convicts, converts, and leads us to grace that we might be holy. "We are his workmanship," says the apostle, "created in Christ Jesus unto good works, which God hath before ordained that we should walk in them" (Ephesians 2:10). And the apostle tells the Christian Thessalonians that God has not called them unto uncleanness but unto holiness (1 Thessalonians 4:7). And again it is written, "As He which hath called you is holy, so be ye holy in all manner of conversation" (1 Peter 1:15).

The spiritual knowledge and understanding that accompany all true grace in the heart promote holy practice. A true knowledge of God and divine things is a practical knowledge. Even wicked people have attained great amounts of speculative knowledge about religion. They may possess vast knowledge of divinity, the Bible, and things pertaining to religion; they may be able to reason very strongly about God's attributes and Christian doctrines; and yet their knowledge fails to be a saving knowledge. It is only speculative and not practical.

He that has a right and saving acquaintance with divine things sees the excellency of holiness and of all the ways of holiness. He sees the beauty and excellency of God, which constitute God's holiness. For the same reason, he sees the hatefulness of sin and of the ways of sin. And if he knows the hatefulness of the ways of sin, certainly he will avoid these ways. If he sees the loveliness of the ways of holiness, he tends to walk in them.

A person who knows God sees that He is worthy to be obeyed. One who has true faith is convinced of the reality and certainty of the great things of faith. One who is convinced of the reality of these things will be influenced by them, and they will govern his actions and behavior. If people are told great things that, if true, intimately concern them, but they do not believe what they are told, they will not be much moved by them. Nor will they alter their conduct based on what they hear. But if they do really believe what they are told, and regard it as certain, they will be influenced by it in their actions and will alter their conduct. We see this in all things of great concern that appear real to people. If a person hears important news that concerns himself and we do not see that he alters his behavior in response, we conclude that he does not believe it is true. We know that human nature is such that we will govern our actions by what we believe and are convinced of.

And so if people are really convinced of the truth of the gospel about an eternal world and the everlasting salvation Christ has purchased, it will influence their practice. They will regulate their behavior according to such a belief so as to obtain this eternal salvation. If people are convinced of the certain truth of the promises of the gospel—eternal riches, honors, and pleasures— and if they really believe these are immensely more valuable than all the riches, honors, and pleasures of the world, they will forsake the things of the world. They will sell all and follow Christ. If they are fully convinced of the truth of the promise that Christ will indeed bestow all these things upon His people, and if all this appears real to them, it will have influence on their practice and it will induce them to live accordingly. Their practice will be according to their convictions.

Human nature forbids that it should be otherwise. If a person is promised by another that if he will part with one pound he will receive a thousand, and if he is fully convinced of the truth of this promise, he will readily part with the former in the assurance of obtaining the latter. And so the one who is convinced of the sufficiency of Christ to deliver him from all evil, and to give him everything that he needs, will be influenced in his practice by the promise which offers him all this. He will not be afraid to believe Christ, even when he might otherwise fear calamity; for he is convinced that Christ is able to deliver him. And so, because he is convinced that Christ alone is sufficient to bestow all happiness upon him, he will not be afraid to forego other ways of securing earthly happiness.

—*All True Grace in the Heart Tends*
to Holy Practice in the Life

QUESTIONS TO CONSIDER

1. What does "holiness" look like in daily life?
2. How does a person become holy?

A PRAYERFUL RESPONSE

Lord, I desire to be holy and blameless before You. Amen.

DAY 26

Sharing in His Suffering

THOUGHT FOR TODAY
A willingness to obey in spite of suffering deepens our
relationship with Christ.

WISDOM FROM SCRIPTURE
Yet whatever gains I had, these I have come to regard as loss
because of Christ.

More than that, I regard everything as loss because of the
surpassing value of knowing Christ Jesus my Lord. For His sake
I have suffered the loss of all things, and I regard them as rub-
bish, in order that I may gain Christ and be found in Him, not
having a righteousness of my own that comes from the law, but
one that comes through faith in Christ, the righteousness from
God based on faith.

I want to know Christ, and the power of His resurrection and
the sharing of His sufferings by becoming like Him in His
death, if somehow I may attain the resurrection from the dead.

Not that I have already obtained this or have already reached
the goal; but I press on to make it my own, because Christ Jesus
has made me His own.

Beloved, I do not consider that I have made it my own; but
this one thing I do: forgetting what lies behind and straining
forward to what lies ahead.

I press on toward the goal for the prize of the heavenly call
of God in Christ Jesus.

PHILIPPIANS 3:7-14, NRSV

Hypocrites may, and oftentimes do, make a great show of religion in profession—in words that cost nothing and in actions that involve no great difficulty or suffering. But they have not a suffering spirit—a spirit that inclines them willingly to suffer for Christ's sake.

When they undertook religion, it was not with any view toward suffering or with any expectation of being injured by it in their temporal interests. They accepted Christ, so far as they did, only to help themselves. All that they do in religious things is from a selfish spirit and for their own interest, as it was with the Pharisees. Therefore they are far, either in their persons or their interests, from the spirit that is willing to meet suffering.

But those who are truly Christians have a spirit to suffer for Christ, and they are willing to follow Him on that condition. And not only are they willing to suffer for Christ; it is also implied in our doctrine that they have the spirit to undergo all the sufferings to which their duty to Christ may expose them. They are willing to undergo all sufferings. They have the spirit of willingness to suffer in their good name, to suffer for Christ's sake reproach and contempt. They prefer the honor of Christ before their own.

They are willing also to undergo all sufferings of all degrees that are in the way of duty. They are like pure gold that will bear the trial of the hottest furnace. They have the heart to forsake all and follow Christ, to comparatively "hate" even "father and mother, and wife, and children, and brethren, and sisters, yea, and their own life also" (Luke 14:26), for Christ's sake.

It is necessary that we as Christians, as followers of Christ, should give ourselves to Him unreservedly, to be His wholly, only, and forever. The believer's coming to Christ is often, in the

Scriptures, compared to the act of a bride giving herself in marriage to her husband. A woman gives herself to her husband in marriage to be his and his alone. True believers are not their own, for they are bought with a price; they consent to Christ's full right to them and recognize it by their own act, giving themselves to Him as a voluntary and living sacrifice, wholly devoted to Him.

Those who do not have a spirit to suffer all things for Christ do not give themselves wholly to Him. In those cases they desire to be excused from suffering for Christ and His glory, and choose rather that His cause should meet their own ease or interest—and indeed should entirely give way to it. But excusing themselves from suffering is certainly inconsistent with truly devoting themselves to God. It is rather like Ananias and Sapphira, who kept back part of that which they professed to give to the Lord.

To give ourselves wholly to Christ implies the sacrificing of our own temporal interests to Him. But he who wholly sacrifices his temporal interests to Christ is ready to suffer all things for Him. If God is truly loved, He is loved as God, and to love Him as God is to love Him as the Supreme Good. But he who loves God as the Supreme Good is ready to make all other good give place to that. He is willing to suffer all for the sake of this good.

It is the character of all true followers of Christ that they follow Him in all things. It is the character of true Christians that they overcome the world. To overcome the world implies that we overcome its flatteries and frowns, its sufferings and difficulties. These are the weapons by which the world seeks to conquer us. If we have not the spirit to encounter such difficulties for

Christ's sake, then by such weapons the world will have us in subjection and will gain the victory over us.

But Christ gives His servants the victory over the world in all its forms. We are conquerors, and more than conquerors, through Him who has loved us. Sufferings in the way of duty are often, in the Bible, called temptations or trials, because by them God tries the sincerity of our character as Christians. By placing such sufferings in our way God tries us, as gold is tried by the fire, to know if it be pure gold or not, to distinguish it from all baser metals and from all imitations of it. Thus does God try our sincerity, to know whether we have a spirit to undergo suffering.

— *Charity Willing to Undergo All Sufferings for Christ*

QUESTIONS TO CONSIDER
1. When have you suffered for the cause of Christ?
2. How was God faithful in that situation?

A PRAYERFUL RESPONSE
Lord, I am willing to obey You, regardless of the cost. Amen.

DAY 27

Many Graces, One Love

THOUGHT FOR TODAY
God's grace and love are rich and interconnected.

WISDOM FROM SCRIPTURE
You were dead through the trespasses and sins in which you once lived, following the course of this world, following the ruler of the power of the air, the spirit that is now at work among those who are disobedient.

All of us once lived among them in the passions of our flesh and senses, and we were by nature children of wrath, like everyone else.

But God, who is rich in mercy, out of the great love with which He loved us even when we were dead through our trespasses, made us alive together with Christ—by grace you have been saved—and raised us up with Him and seated us with Him in the heavenly places in Christ Jesus, so that in the ages to come He might show the immeasurable riches of his grace in kindness toward us in Christ Jesus.

For by grace you have been saved through faith, and this is not your own doing; it is the gift of God—not the result of works, so that no one may boast.

EPHESIANS 2:1-9, NRSV

The graces of Christianity are all interconnected and mutually dependent on each other. That is, they are all linked together and united one to another and within one another, like the links of a chain. One link hangs on another, from one end of the chain to the other, so that if one link is broken, all fall to the ground, and the whole ceases to be of any effect.

The graces so go together that where there is one, there are all, and where one is wanting, all are wanting. Where there is faith, there is love, hope, and humility; and where there is love, there is also trust. Where there is a holy trust in God, there is love for God. Where there is a gracious hope, there also is a holy fear of God. Where there is love for God, there is a gracious love for others. Where there is a Christian love for others, there is love for God.

There is not only a connection whereby these graces are always joined together, but there is also a mutual dependence between them, so that one cannot exist without the others. To deny one would in effect be to deny another, and thus all of them—just as to deny the cause would be to deny the effect, or to deny the effect would be to deny the cause.

Faith promotes love, and love is the most effectual ingredient in a living faith. Love is dependent on faith, for a being cannot be truly loved, and especially loved above all other beings, who is not looked upon as a real being. And then love, again, enlarges and promotes faith, because we are more likely to believe, give credit to, and trust in those we love than in those we do not.

So faith begets hope, for faith sees and trusts in both God's sufficiency to bestow blessings and in His faithfulness to His promises—that He will do what He has said. All gracious hope is hope resting on faith, and hope encourages and draws forth acts of faith. And in like manner love promotes hope, for the spirit of love is the spirit of a child; and the more anyone feels in himself this spirit toward God, the more natural it will be for him to look to God and go to God as his Father. This childlike spirit casts out the spirit of bondage and fear and replaces it with the Spirit of adoption, which is the spirit of confidence and hope. And so, again, a true and genuine hope tends greatly to promote love.

Faith, too, promotes humility; for the more entirely anyone depends on God's sufficiency, the more will he tend toward a low sense of his own sufficiency. In like manner, humility promotes faith. The more sense anyone has of his insufficiency, the more will his heart be disposed to trust only in God and depend entirely on Christ. On the other hand, love promotes humility; for the more the heart is ravished with God's loveliness, the more will it abhor, abase, and humble itself for its own unloveliness and vileness.

Humility also promotes love, for the more sense anyone has of his unworthiness, the more will he admire God's goodness to him, and the more will his heart be drawn out in love for God in response to His glorious grace. Love promotes repentance, for he who truly repents of sin repents of it because it is committed against a being whom he loves. And repentance promotes humility; for no one can be truly sorry for sin, and self-condemned in view of it, without being humbled in heart.

Repentance, faith, and love—all promote thankfulness. He who by faith trusts in Christ for salvation will be thankful to Him for that salvation. He who loves God will be disposed thankfully to acknowledge His kindness. And he who repents of his sins will be disposed heartily to thank God for the grace that is sufficient to deliver him from sin's guilt and power. A true love for God promotes love for those who bear the image of God; and a spirit of love and peace toward others cherishes a spirit of love for God.

So it might be shown by mentioning many other particulars how all the graces depend one upon another. Humility cherishes all other graces, and all other graces promote humility; faith promotes all other graces, and all other graces cherish and promote faith. And the like is true of every one of the graces of the gospel.

The different graces of Christianity are in some respects implied one in another. They are not only mutually interconnected and dependent but in some respects implied in the nature of each other. In respect to several of them, one is essential to another, belonging to its very essence. Thus, for example, humility is implied in the nature of true faith; humility is of the essence of faith. It is essential to a true faith that it be humble. In like manner, humility belongs to the nature and essence of many other true graces. It is essential to Christian love that it be humble love; to submission, that it be humble submission; to repentance, that it be humble repentance; to thankfulness, that it be humble thankfulness; and to reverence, that it be humble reverence.

And so is love implied in a gracious faith. It is an ingredient of it, belongs to its essence, and is the very soul of it—of its working, operative nature. As the working, operative nature of a person is his soul, so the working and operative nature of faith is love. The apostle Paul tells us that "faith worketh by love" (Galatians 5:6); and the apostle James tells us that faith without its working nature is dead, as the body is without the spirit (James 2:26). And so faith is in some respects implied in love, for it is essential to a true Christian love that it be a believing love.

Likewise, saving repentance and faith are implied in each other. They are both one and the same conversion of the soul from sin to God, through Christ. The act of the soul in turning from sin to God through Christ is called repentance. The mediation by which it turns is called faith. But it is the same motion of the soul, like a person turning and fleeing from darkness to the light.

Love is implied, too, in thankfulness. True thankfulness is no other than the exercise of love for God because of His goodness to us. And there is love in a true and childlike fear of God. Childlike fear differs from a slavish fear, for a slavish fear has no love in it. And all these three graces of love, humility, and repentance are implied in gracious, childlike submission to the will of God.

And so weaning oneself from the world is accomplished mainly by the three graces of faith, hope, and love. Christian love for others is a kind of mediate, or indirect, love for Christ; and justice and truth, which are surely Christian graces, have love in them.

—All the Christian Graces Connected
and Mutually Dependent

QUESTIONS TO CONSIDER

1. How do faith and humility work together with grace and love in your life?
2. When one component is missing, what are the effects?

A PRAYERFUL RESPONSE

Lord, teach me the depth of Your grace and love. Amen.

DAY 28

Love Lasts

THOUGHT FOR TODAY
God's love is eternal.

WISDOM FROM SCRIPTURE
What then are we to say about these things? If God is for us, who is against us?

He who did not withhold his own Son, but gave him up for all of us, will he not with him also give us everything else?

Who will bring any charge against God's elect? It is God who justifies.

Who is to condemn? It is Christ Jesus, who died, yes, who was raised, who is at the right hand of God, who indeed intercedes for us.

Who will separate us from the love of Christ? Will hardship, or distress, or persecution, or famine, or nakedness, or peril, or sword?

As it is written, "For your sake we are being killed all day long; we are accounted as sheep to be slaughtered."

No, in all these things we are more than conquerors through him who loved us.

For I am convinced that neither death, nor life, nor angels, nor rulers, nor things present, nor things to come, nor powers, nor height, nor depth, nor anything else in all creation, will be able to separate us from the love of God in Christ Jesus our Lord.

ROMANS 8:31-39, NRSV

Many things greatly oppose the grace of true charity that dwells in the heart of the Christian. This holy principle has innumerable enemies watching and warring against it. The child of God is encompassed with enemies on every side. He is a pilgrim and stranger passing through an enemy's country, exposed to attack at any moment. There are thousands of devils—artful, intelligent, active, mighty, and implacable—that are bitter enemies to the grace that dwells in the heart of the Christian; and they do all that lies in their power against it.

The world is also an enemy to this grace, because the world abounds with persons and things that oppose it, and that with various forms of allurement and temptation attempt to drive us from the path of duty. And the Christian has not only many enemies outside himself but multitudes within his own breast— enemies that he carries about with him and from which he cannot get free. Evil thoughts and sinful inclinations cling to him. The many corruptions that still hold their footing in his heart are the worst enemies of grace and have the greatest advantage of any in their warfare against it.

These enemies are not only many but exceedingly strong and powerful, and very bitter in their animosity. They are implacable, irreconcilable, mortal enemies, seeking nothing short of the utter ruin and overthrow of grace. And they are so unwearied in their opposition that the Christian, while he remains in this world, is always in a state of warfare, and his business is that of the soldier. Indeed, he is often spoken of as a soldier of the cross and as one whose great duty it is to fight the good fight of faith.

Many are the powerful and violent assaults that the enemies of grace make upon it. They are not only constantly besieging it, but often they assault it like a city that they would take by storm. They are always lurking and watching for opportunity against it, and sometimes they rise up in dreadful wrath and endeavor to overcome it by urgent assault: sometimes one enemy, sometimes another, and sometimes all together with one consent, buffeting it on every side, coming in like a flood, ready to overwhelm it and swallow it up at once.

In the midst of the most violent opposition of the enemies that fight against it with united subtlety and strength, grace is like a spark of fire encompassed with swelling billows and raging waves that threaten to swallow it up and extinguish it in a moment. Or it is like a flake of snow falling into a burning volcano, or a rich jewel of gold in the midst of a fiery furnace, its raging heat enough to consume anything except the pure gold, which cannot be consumed by fire.

Grace in the heart of a Christian is very much like the church of God in the world: it is God's post, though a small one. Like the church, it is opposed by innumerable enemies. The powers of earth and hell are engaged against it—if possible, to destroy it. Oftentimes they rise with such violence and come with such great strength against it that if we were to judge only by what we see, we should think it would be destroyed immediately.

Grace in a Christian's heart is also like the children of Israel in Egypt, against whom Pharaoh and the Egyptians united all their craft and power to exterminate them as a people. It is like David in the wilderness, hunted as a partridge on the mountains, driven from one desert or cave to another and several times chased into a strange land by those who sought his life. And it is like the Christian church under the heathen and anti-Christian persecutions, when all the world united its strength to exterminate it from the earth—and without respect to sex or age, with the utmost cruelty and by the most bloody persecutions, destroyed millions.

Yet all the opposition that is or can be made against true grace in the heart cannot overthrow it. The enemies of grace may, in many respects, gain great advantages against it; they may exceedingly oppress and reduce it, and bring it into such circumstances that it may seem to be brought to the brink of utter ruin. But still it will live. The ruin that seemed impending shall be averted.

Though the roaring lion sometimes comes with open mouth, and no visible refuge appears, yet the lamb shall escape and be safe. Though it be in the very paw of the lion or bear, yet it shall be rescued and not devoured. And though it seems actually swallowed down, as Jonah was by the whale, yet it shall be brought up again and live. Grace in the heart, in this respect, is like the ark upon the waters, however terrible the storm may be. Though it overwhelms everything else, yet it shall not overwhelm that. Though the floods rise ever so high, yet it shall be kept above the waters; and though the mighty waves may rise above the tops of the highest mountains, yet they shall not be able to get above this ark; it shall still float in safety.

And grace shall not only remain, but it shall in the end have the victory. Though it may pass through a long time of sore conflicts and may suffer many disadvantages and depressions, yet it shall live—and not only live, but prosper and prevail and triumph, for all its enemies shall be subdued under its feet. Where grace truly exists in the heart, all its enemies cannot destroy it, and all the opposition made against it cannot crush it. It endures all things, withstands all shocks, and persists in spite of all opposers.

—Charity, or True Grace, Not to Be
Overthrown by Opposition

QUESTIONS TO CONSIDER

1. Do you ever feel separated from God's love and grace? Why?
2. How could you reaffirm that God's love and grace still abide with you?

A PRAYERFUL RESPONSE

Lord, thank You for Your everlasting love and grace. Amen.

DAY 29

The Spirit of Love

THOUGHT FOR TODAY

God and His love dwell in us through the Holy Spirit.

WISDOM FROM SCRIPTURE

If you love Me, you will keep My commandments.

And I will ask the Father, and he will give you another Advocate, to be with you forever.

This is the Spirit of truth, whom the world cannot receive, because it neither sees Him nor knows Him. You know Him, because He abides with you, and He will be in you.

I will not leave you orphaned; I am coming to you.

In a little while the world will no longer see me, but you will see me; because I live, you also will live.

I have said these things to you while I am still with you.

But the Advocate, the Holy Spirit, whom the Father will send in My name, will teach you everything, and remind you of all that I have said to you.

JOHN 14:15-19, 25-26, NRSV

INSIGHTS FROM JONATHAN EDWARDS

The knowledge that Christians have of God and Christ and spiritual things shall not vanish away but shall be gloriously increased and perfected in heaven, which is a world of light and love. The Spirit of Christ is given to His church and people everlastingly, to influence and to dwell in them. The Holy Spirit is the great purchase—that is, the purchased gift—of Christ: the chief and sum of all the good things in this life and in the life to come that Christ purchased for the church. And just as the Spirit of Christ is the great purchase, so He is also the great promise, the great thing promised by God and Christ to the church, as the apostle Peter made clear on the day of Pentecost (Acts 2:32, 33).

This great purchase and promise of Christ is forever to be given to His church. He has promised that His church shall continue; He expressly declared that the gates of hell shall not prevail against it. And in order that it may be preserved, He has given his Holy Spirit to every true member of it and promised the continuance of that Spirit forever. His own language is, "And I will pray the Father, and He shall give you another Comforter, that He may abide with you forever; even the Spirit of truth; whom the world cannot receive, because it seeth Him not, neither knoweth Him: but ye know Him; for He dwelleth with you, and shall be in you" (John 14:16-17).

Humans, in their first estate in Eden, had the Holy Spirit but lost it by their disobedience. But God has provided a way for the Spirit to be restored, and now it is given to the saints a second time, never more to depart from us, and in such a way as to become truly ours.

The Spirit of God was given to and dwelt with our first parents in their state of innocence, but not in the same sense in which He is now given to and dwells within Christians. Our first parents had no proper right or sure title to the Spirit, and it was not finally and forever given to them in the way it is to believers in Christ.

But the Spirit of Christ is not only *communicated* to those who are converted; He is *given over* to them by a sure covenant, so that He becomes their own. Christ becomes theirs, and therefore His fullness is theirs, and therefore His Spirit is their purchased, promised, and sure possession.

—The Holy Spirit Forever to Be Communicated
to the Saints, in Charity, or Love

QUESTIONS TO CONSIDER

1. How has Jesus purchased the Holy Spirit for us?
2. What difference does the Holy Spirit make in our daily lives?

A PRAYERFUL RESPONSE

Lord, thank You for the gift of Your indwelling Spirit. Amen.

Heaven, a World of Love

THOUGHT FOR TODAY
God has saved the best place for last.

WISDOM FROM SCRIPTURE

Then the angel showed me the river of the water of life, bright as crystal, flowing from the throne of God and of the Lamb through the middle of the street of the city. On either side of the river is the tree of life with its twelve kinds of fruit, producing its fruit each month; and the leaves of the tree are for the healing of the nations.

Nothing accursed will be found there any more. But the throne of God and of the Lamb will be in it, and His servants will worship Him; they will see His face, and His name will be on their foreheads.

And there will be no more night; they need no light of lamp or sun, for the Lord God will be their light, and they will reign forever and ever.

And He said to me, "These words are trustworthy and true, for the Lord, the God of the spirits of the prophets, has sent His angel to show His servants what must soon take place.

"See, I am coming soon! Blessed is the one who keeps the words of the prophecy of this book."

REVELATION 22:1-7, NRSV

The heavenly state of the church is distinguished from its earthly state. God has designed heaven for direct communication with His Holy Spirit. In heaven the Spirit shall be given perfectly, whereas in the present state of the church, He is given with great imperfection.

In the heavenly state of the church, holy love or charity shall be the only gift or fruit of the Spirit—the most perfect and glorious gift of all. Being brought to perfection, love renders unnecessary all other gifts that God bestowed on His church on earth.

Heaven is the palace or presence-chamber of the High and Holy One whose name is love, and who is both the cause and source of all holy love. God, considered with respect to His essence, is everywhere—He fills both heaven and earth. Yet He is said, in some respects, to be more especially in some places than in others. He was said of old to dwell in the land of Israel, above all other lands; and in Jerusalem, above all other cities of that land; and in the temple, above all other buildings in the city; and in the Holy of Holies, above all other apartments of the temple; and on the mercy seat over the ark of the covenant, above all other places in the Holy of Holies.

But heaven is His dwelling place above all other places in the universe; and all those places in which He was said to dwell of old were only types of heaven. Heaven is a part of creation that God has built for one end: to be the place of His glorious presence. It is His abode forever, and there will He dwell and gloriously manifest Himself throughout all eternity.

And this renders heaven a world of love; for God is the fountain of love, as the sun is the fountain of light. The glorious presence of God in heaven fills heaven with love in the same way the sun, placed in the midst of the visible heavens on a clear day, fills the world with light. The apostle tells us that "God is love" (1 John 4:8). Therefore, seeing that He is an infinite being, it follows that He is an infinite fountain of love. Seeing that He is an all-sufficient being, it follows that He is a full and overflowing—an inexhaustible—fountain of love. And in that He is an unchangeable and eternal being, He is an unchangeable and eternal fountain of love.

There, even in heaven, dwells the God from whom every stream of holy love, every drop that is or ever was, proceeds. There dwells God the Father, God the Son, and God the Spirit, united as one in infinitely dear, incomprehensible, mutual, and eternal love.

There dwells God the Father, who is the Father of mercies and so the Father of love, who so loved the world He gave his only-begotten Son to die for it. There dwells Christ, the Lamb of God, the Prince of Peace and of love, who so loved the world that He shed his blood and poured out His soul unto death for humanity. There dwells the great Mediator, through whom divine love is expressed toward humans, and by whom the fruits of that love have been purchased, and through whom they are communicated, and through whom love is imparted to the hearts of all God's people.

There dwells Christ in both His natures, the human and the divine, sitting on the same throne with the Father. And there dwells the Holy Spirit, the Spirit of divine love, in whom the very essence of God flows out and is breathed forth in love, and by whose immediate influence all holy love is shed abroad in the hearts of all the saints on earth and in heaven.

There, in heaven, this infinite fountain of love flows forever. There this glorious God is manifested, and shines forth in full glory, in beams of love. And there this glorious fountain forever flows forth in streams and rivers of love and delight. These rivers swell to an ocean of love, in which the souls of the ransomed may bathe with the sweetest enjoyment, and their hearts are deluged with love!

The great God who so fully manifests himself in heaven is perfect with an absolute and infinite perfection. The Son of God, who is the brightness of the Father's glory, appears there in the fullness of His glory. The Holy Ghost shall be poured forth there with perfect richness and sweetness, like a pure river of the water of life, clear as crystal, proceeding out of the throne of God and of the Lamb. And every member of that holy and blessed society shall be without any stain of sin, or imperfection or weakness or imprudence or blemish of any kind. The whole church, ransomed and purified, shall there be presented to Christ as a bride, clothed in fine linen, clean and white, without spot or wrinkle.

Wherever the inhabitants of that blessed world shall turn their eyes, they shall see nothing but dignity, beauty, and glory. The most stately cities on earth, however magnificent their buildings, have their foundations in the dust, and their streets are dirty and defiled, made to be trodden underfoot. But the very streets of this heavenly city are of pure gold, like transparent glass, and its foundations are of precious stones, and its gates are pearl. And all these are but faint emblems of the purity and perfection of those who dwell within.

Christ loves all His saints in heaven. His love flows out to His whole church there, and to every individual member of it. And they all, with one heart and one soul, unite in love to their common Redeemer. Every heart is wedded to this holy and spiritual husband, and all the saints rejoice in Him, and the angels join them in their love. The angels and the saints all love each other; all the members of the glorious society of heaven are sincerely united. There is not a single secret or open enemy among them all. Not a heart is there that is not full of love; not a solitary inhabitant who is not beloved by all the others. And as all are lovely, so all see each other's loveliness with full security and delight. Every soul goes out in love to every other; and among all the blessed inhabitants, love is mutual and full and eternal.

—*Heaven, a World of Love*

QUESTIONS TO CONSIDER

1. Are you prepared to spend eternity in heaven?
2. If not, how can you know you're ready?

A PRAYERFUL RESPONSE

Lord, I long for the day when I am with You always. Amen.

JONATHAN EDWARDS' RESOLUTIONS
(1722–1723)

Knowing I am unable to do anything without God's help, I humbly entreat Him by His grace to enable me to keep these Resolutions, so far as they are agreeable to His will, for Christ's sake.

1. Resolved, that I will do whatever I think to be best for God's glory and my own good, profit, and pleasure, without any consideration of the time. Resolved to do whatever I think to be my duty for the good and advantage of humanity in general. Resolved to do this, whatever difficulties I meet with.

2. Resolved, to be continually endeavoring to find out some new invention and contrivance to promote the aforementioned things.

3. Resolved, if ever I shall fall and grow dull so as to neglect to keep any part of these Resolutions, to repent of all I can remember when I come to myself again.

4. Resolved, never to do any manner of thing, whether in soul or body, except what tends to the glory of God.

5. Resolved, never to lose one moment of time, but to improve it in the most profitable way I possibly can.

6. Resolved, to live with all my might while I do live.

7. Resolved, never to do anything that I should be afraid to do if it were the last hour of my life.

8. Resolved, to act in all respects, both in speaking and doing, as if I had committed the same sins or had the same failings as others; and to let the knowledge of their failings promote nothing but shame in myself, and prove only an occasion of confessing my own sins and misery to God.

9. Resolved, to think much on all occasions about my own dying, and about the common circumstances which attend death.

10. Resolved, when I feel pain, to think of the pains of martyrdom and of hell.

11. Resolved, when I think of any theorem in divinity to be solved, immediately to do what I can towards solving it, if circumstances do not hinder me.

12. Resolved, if I take delight in any such solution as a gratification of pride or vanity, or on any such account, immediately to throw it away.

13. Resolved, to endeavor to find out fit recipients of charity and liberality.

14. Resolved, never to do anything out of revenge.

15. Resolved, never to suffer the least motions of anger to irrational beings.

16. Resolved, never upon any account to speak evil of anyone so that it shall tend to his dishonor, except for some real good.

17. Resolved, that I will live so as I shall wish I had done when I come to die.

18. Resolved, to live at all times as I think is best when I am in my most devout frame of mind and when I understand most clearly the things of the gospel.

19. Resolved, never to do anything that I should be afraid to do if I should expect to hear the last trump within the hour.

20. Resolved, to maintain the strictest temperance in eating and drinking.

21. Resolved, never to do anything that, if I should see it in another, I should despise him for or in any way think less of him.

22. Resolved, to endeavor to obtain for myself as much happiness in the other world as I possibly can, with all the power, might, vigor, and vehemence—yea, even violence—of which I am capable.

23. Resolved, frequently to take some deliberate action for the glory of God that seems least likely to be done, and trace it back to the original intention, designs, and ends of it; and if I find it not to be for God's glory, to repute it as a breach of the fourth Resolution.

24. Resolved, whenever I do any conspicuously evil action, to trace it back till I come to the original cause; and then to carefully endeavor not to do it again, and to fight and pray with all my might against it.

25. Resolved, to examine carefully and constantly what that one thing in me is which causes me to doubt the love of God; and to direct all my forces against it.

26. Resolved, to cast away the things that abate my assurance.

27. Resolved, never willfully to omit anything, unless the omission be for the glory of God; and frequently to examine my omissions.

28. Resolved, to study the Scriptures so steadily, constantly, and frequently that I may grow in the knowledge of the same.

29. Resolved, never to count that which I cannot hope God will answer as a prayer, nor let it pass as a prayer or petition; nor count as a confession that which I cannot hope God will accept.

30. Resolved, to strive to my utmost every week to be brought higher in my faith and to a higher exercise of grace than I was the week before.

31. Resolved, never to say anything against anybody, except when it is perfectly agreeable to the highest degree of Christian honor and love, agreeable to the lowest humility and sense of my own faults and failings, and agreeable to the Golden Rule; and when I have said anything against anyone, to bring it to the test of this Resolution.

32. Resolved, to be strictly and firmly faithful to my trust so that Proverbs 20:6, "A faithful man, who can find?" may be fulfilled in me.

33. Resolved, always to do what I can toward making, maintaining, establishing, and preserving peace when it can be done without detriment in other respects.

34. Resolved, in narrations never to speak anything but the pure and simple truth.

35. Resolved, whenever I question whether I have done my duty to such a degree that my quiet and calm is disturbed, to write it down, along with how my questions were then resolved.

36. Resolved, never to speak evil of any, unless I have some particular good call for it.

37. Resolved, to inquire every night as I am going to bed how I have been negligent, what sin I have committed, and how I have denied myself; also at the end of every week, month, and year.

38. Resolved, never to speak anything that is ridiculous, sportive, or a matter of laughter on the Lord's Day.

39. Resolved, never to do anything about which I question the lawfulness, unless I question the lawfulness of the omission to the same degree.

40. Resolved, to inquire every night before I go to bed whether I have acted in the best way I possibly could with respect to eating and drinking.

41. Resolved, to ask myself at the end of every day, week, month, and year, wherein I could have done better.

42. Resolved, frequently to renew the dedication of myself to God made at my baptism, which I solemnly renewed when I was received into the communion of the church, and which I have solemnly re-made this twelfth day of January, 1723.

43. Resolved, never henceforward till I die, to act as if I were in any way my own, but entirely and altogether God's, agreeable to what is to be found herein this Saturday, January 12, 1723.

44. Resolved, that no other end but my faith in God shall have any influence at all on any of my actions.

45. Resolved, never to allow myself any pleasure or grief, joy or sorrow, nor any affection at all, nor any degree of affection, nor any circumstance relating to it, except what helps my faith in God.

46. Resolved, never to allow myself the least measure of any uneasy fretting at my father or mother. Resolved to display no indication of fault-finding, not even the least alteration of my speech or motion of my eye; and to be especially careful with respect to any of our family.

47. Resolved, to endeavor to my utmost to deny whatever is not most agreeable to a good, universally sweet and benevolent, quiet, peaceable, contented, easy, compassionate, generous, humble, meek, modest, submissive, obliging, diligent and industrious, charitable, even, patient, moderate, forgiving, sincere temper; and to do at all times what such a temper would lead me to. Examine strictly every week whether I have done so.

48. Resolved, constantly, with the utmost care and diligence and the strictest scrutiny, to be looking into the state of my soul, that I may know whether I have truly an interest in Christ or not; that when I come to die, I may not have any negligence respecting this of which to repent.

49. Resolved, that if I can help it, this never shall be.

50. Resolved, I will act in such a manner as I think I shall judge, when I come into the future world, would have been best and most prudent.

51. Resolved, that I will act in every respect in the manner I think I shall wish I had done if I should in the end be damned.

52. I frequently hear persons in old age say how they would live, if they were to live their lives over again: Resolved, that I will live exactly in the manner I think I shall wish I had done, supposing I live to old age.

53. Resolved, to improve every opportunity, when I am in the best and happiest frame of mind, to cast and venture my soul on the Lord Jesus Christ, to trust and confide in Him, and to consecrate myself wholly to Him; that from this I may have assurance of my safety, knowing that I confide in my Redeemer.

54. Resolved, whenever I hear anything spoken in conversation of any person, if I think it praiseworthy, to endeavor to imitate it.

55. Resolved, to endeavor to my utmost to act in such a manner as I think I should do if I had already seen the happiness of heaven and the torments of hell.

56. Resolved, never to give up nor in the least to slacken my fight with my corruptions, however unsuccessful I may be.

57. Resolved, when I fear misfortunes and adversities, to examine whether I have yet done my duty and to resolve to do it; and as providence orders it, so far as I am able, to be concerned about nothing but my duty and my sin.

58. Resolved, not only to refrain from an air of dislike, fretfulness, and anger in conversation, but to exhibit an air of love and cheerfulness.

59. Resolved, when I am most conscious of provocations to ill nature and anger, that I will strive most to feel and act good-naturedly; and at such times to manifest good nature even should I think that in other respects and at other times it would be disadvantageous or imprudent.

60. Resolved, whenever my feelings begin to appear in the least out of order, when I am conscious of the least uneasiness within or the least irregularity without, that I will subject myself to the strictest examination.

61. Resolved, that I will not give way to that listlessness which I find unbends and relaxes my mind from being fully and fixedly set on faith in God.

62. Resolved, never to do anything but duty; and then according to Ephesians 6:6-8 to do it willingly and cheerfully as unto the Lord, and not to man: "knowing that whatever good thing any man doth, the same shall he receive of the Lord."

63. Resolved, on the supposition that there might be only one individual in the world at any one time who was properly a complete Christian, to act just as I would do if I strove with all my might to be that one in my time.

64. Resolved, that when I find those "groanings which cannot be uttered" (Romans 8:26) of which the apostle speaks, and those "breakings of soul for the longing it hath" (Psalm 119:20) of which the Psalmist speaks, I will promote them to the utmost of my power.

65. Resolved, all my life long, with the greatest openness of which I am capable, to declare my ways to God and lay open my soul to Him: all my sins, temptations, difficulties, sorrows, fears, hopes, desires, and every thing and circumstance.

66. Resolved, that I will endeavor always to keep a kind and gracious disposition, in all places and in all companies, unless duty requires otherwise.

67. Resolved, after afflictions, to inquire how I am the better for them, what good I have got by them, and what I might have got by them.

68. Resolved, to confess frankly to myself all that I find in myself of either infirmity or sin; and if it be what concerns my faith, also to confess the whole case to God, and to implore needed help.

69. Resolved, always to do that which I shall wish I had done when I see others do it.

70. Let there be something of benevolence in all that I speak.

SERMONS BY JONATHAN EDWARDS

Many of Jonathan Edwards' sermons appear
on the World Wide Web at:

http://www.jonathanedwards.com/

ABOUT THE COMPILERS

With the Life Messages devotional series, **Judith Couchman** hopes you'll be encouraged and enlightened by people who have shared their spiritual journeys through the printed word.

Judith owns Judith & Company, a writing and editing business. She has also served as the creator and founding editor-in-chief of *Clarity* magazine, managing editor of *Christian Life,* editor of *Sunday Digest,* director of communications for The Navigators, and director of new product development for the periodicals division of NavPress.

Besides speaking to women's and professional groups, Judith is the author or compiler of 40 books and many magazine articles. She also founded and directs the "Write the Vision" Retreats for women who want to write for publication. In addition, she has received numerous awards for her work in secondary education, religious publishing, and corporate communications. She lives in Colorado.

Lisa Marzano is Director of Special Projects for International Students Incorporated and a freelance writer. She spends much of her time organizing large conferences and events. Lisa lives in Colorado.